DATE DUE

NOV 30 '92			

The International Trade Union Movement

by Prof. J. P. Windmuller

This book was originally published as a monograph in the
International Encyclopaedia for Labour Law and Industrial Relations

1980

KLUWER
DEVENTER/BOSTON/LONDON/FRANKFURT/
ANTWERP

Distribution in the USA

Kluwer Law and Taxation Publishers
190, Old Derby Street
Hingham, MA 02043
USA

Library of Congress Cataloging in Publication Data

Windmuller, John P.
International Trade Union Movement.
Bibliography: p.
Includes index.
1. International labor activities. I. Title.
HD6475.A1W548 331.88'091 80-13814

ISBN 90 312 0121 9

D/1980/2664/25

Cover design: Pieter J. van der Sman

Introduction

Although trade unions are essentially national institutions functioning within nationally determined rules, they have for about a century maintained international associations for cooperation and mutual support. Of course until World War I the international dimension of trade unionism was, in effect, confined to Europe where the trade unions shared, by and large, a common ideological outlook, similar problems of organization, and more or less the same difficulties in dealings with employers and the state. Awareness of these common elements led to the creation of modest international associations for limited practical objectives within a democratic socialist perspective.

The socialist worldview perceived capitalism as an international phenomenon which required a countervailing force on the worker side. But a sober perception of the limited possibilities for international action defined the tasks of that countervailing force in relatively simple terms: exchanges of information about pay and working conditions, mutual support in times of industrial conflict, unchallenged union membership transfers for migrants and travelling members, and occasional declarations of protest against particularly flagrant anti-labor policies of governments and employers.

Two basic types of international trade union organization emerged during the formative years just before and after the turn of the century. One consisted of unions from different countries in distinct crafts and occupations: printers, miners, hatters, leather workers, and various others. These groupings became known as International Trade Secretariats, a designation still in use today even though the organizations concerned are no longer composed of unions for individual trades, as used to be the case, but instead of unions claiming jurisdiction over entire industries or major economic sectors. (In other words, if the nomenclature had kept in step with changing conditions, we would now probably call them International Industry Secretariats.)

The other basic type united the national trade union centers or federations from different countries in a confederal group which eventually took the name of International Federation of Trade Unions. While the Secretariats devoted their attention mainly to the specific problems associated with a particular occupation, and later with a particular industry or economic sector, the differently constituted confederation of national trade union centers took the initiative on broader issues of social and economic policy, international labor legislation, and major political developments of concern to workers of all kinds. This division of labor has remained in effect to the present day.

During the interwar period, the structure of international trade unionism became more complicated. The socialist-oriented formations established during the prewar period reconstructed their ranks along familiar patterns, but they now faced competition from two new forces: an international grouping of trade unions inspired by the Christian social ethic and held together by an International Federation of Christian Trade Unions, and an organization of Communist labor bodies loyal to the Soviet Union and united in the Red International of Labor Unions. In the Western hemisphere several regional trade union bodies came into existence as independent organizations.

These new divisions, based on ideology and regional separatism, were temporarily thought not fully overcome during the years immediately after the Second World War when international labor unity appeared to be an attainable objective. Eventually, however, they reasserted themselves. In the contemporary world, ideology and regional attachment have again become the chief determinants of the international trade union structure, and this study has had to take that situation into account. Chapters I, II and III trace the evolution of international trade union organizations from its simple beginnings to the complex present. The following three chapters (IV, V and VI) review each of the three major contemporary groups: the International Confederation of Free Trade Unions, the World Federation of Trade Unions, and the World Confederation of Labor. Chapter VII examines regional trade union bodies that have been formed independently of the three major tendencies. Finally, Chapter VIII reviews the undramatic but increasingly important activities of the International Trade Secretariats.

Most of the organizations, past and present, that constitute the international trade union movement are not well known. It has, therefore, been necessary to set out in some detail the reasons for their establishment, their internal workings, the tasks which they have set themselves, and their links with other organizations. Although there is no need to inflate their importance, some of them play a significant role in fostering the emergence of trade unions in less developed areas, promoting the extension of human and trade union rights, coordinating trade union efforts to cope with multinational companies, and representing labor interests before intergovernmental bodies of a worldwide or regional character. They deserve more attention than they have heretofore received.

This study was originally prepared as a volume in the *International Encyclopaedia for Labour Law and Industrial Relations*. The author is indebted to the publisher and to the editor-in-chief, Professor Roger Blanpain, for allowing it to appear as a separate publication.

J.P.W.

Table of Contents

Table of Contents

Table of Contents

Abbreviations in Common Use

AAFLI	Asian-American Free Labor Institute (AFL-CIO)
AALC	African-American Labor Center (AFL-CIO)
AATUF	All-African Trade Union Federation
AFL	American Federation of Labor
AFL-CIO	American Federation of Labor-Congress of Industrial Organizations
AFRO	African Regional Organization (ICFTU)
AIFLD	American Institute for Free Labor Development (AFL-CIO)
ARO	Asian Regional Organization (ICFTU)
ATLAS	Agrupación de Trabajadores Latino Americanos Sindicalistas
ATUC	African Trade Union Confederation
AUCCTU	All Union Central Council of Trade Unions (USSR)
BATU	Brotherhood of Asian Trade Unionists (WCL)
CFDT	Confédération Française Démocratique du Travail (French Democratic Confederation of Labor)
CFTC	Confédération Française des Travailleurs Chrétiens (French Confederation of Christian Workers)
CGIL	Confederazione Generale Italiana del Lavoro (General Confederation of Labor)
CGT	Confédération Générale du Travail (French General Confederation of Labor)
CGT-FO	Confédération Générale du Travail-Force Ouvrière (General Confederation of Labor-Workers Force)
CIO	Congress of Industrial Organizations
CISC	Confédération Internationale des Syndicats Chrétiens (International Federation of Christian Trade Unions)
CISL	Confederazione Italiana Sindicati dei Lavoratori (Italian Confederation of Workers' Unions)
CIT	Confederación Interamericana de Trabajadores (Inter-American Confederation of Labor)
CLASC	Confederación Latinoamericana de Syndicalistas Christianos (Latin American Federation of Christian Trade Unionists)
CLAT	Central Latino Americana de Trabajadores (Latin American Workers Center – WCL)
CNV	Christelijk Nationaal Vakverbond (Netherlands Protestant National Trade Union Federation)
COTPAL	Permanent Technical Committee on Labor Matters (OAS)
COSATE	Trade Union Technical Advisory Council (OAS)

Abbreviations in Common Use

CPUSTAL	Congresso Permanente de Unidad Sindical de Trabajadores de America Latina (Permanent Congress of the Unity of Latin American Workers)
CROM	Confederación Regional Obrera Mexicana
CSC	Confédération des Syndicats Chrétiens de Belgique
CTAL	Confederación de Trabajadores de América Latina (Latin American Confederation of Workers)
CTM	Confederación de Trabajadores de Mexico
CUTAL	Central Unica de Trabajadores de América Latina (Latin American Trade Union Center)
DAG	Deutsche Angestellten Gewerkschaft (German White Collar Employees Trade Union)
DGB	Deutscher Gewerkschaftsbund (German Federation of Trade Unions)
DOMEI	Japanese Confederation of Labor
ECFTU	European Confederation of Free Trade Unions
EFTA-TUC	Trade Union Committee in the European Free Trade Area
EITUC	Emergency International Trade Union Council
EMF	European Metalworkers' Federation
EO	European Organization (WCL)
ERO	European Regional Organization (ICFTU)
ETUC	European Trade Union Confederation
FIET	International Federation of Commercial, Clerical and Technical Employees
FGTB	Fédération Générale du Travail de Belgique
FNV	Federatie Nederlandse Vakbeweging (Federation of the Netherlands Trade Union Movement)
FOPADESC	Fondation Panafricaine pour le Développement Economique, Social et Culturel (WCL)
GFTU	General Federation of Trade Unions of Great Britain
ICATU	International Confederation of Arab Trade Unions
ICEF	International Federation of Chemical, Energy, and General Workers Unions
ICFTU	International Confederation of Free Trade Unions
IFBWW	International Federation of Building and Woodworkers
IFPAAW	International Federation of Plantation, Agricultural and Allied Workers
IFPCW	International Federation of Petroleum and Chemical Workers
IFTU	International Federation of Trade Unions
IGF	International Graphical Federation
IMF	International Metalworkers Federation
ISF	International Solidarity Fund (ICFTU)
ITD	International Trade Department (WFTU)
ITS	International Transport Workers' Federation

ITGLWF	International Textile, Garment and Leather Workers' Federation
ITS	International Trade Secretariat
IUF	International Union of Food and Allied Workers' Associations
IWW	Industrial Workers of the World
LSI	Labor and Socialist International
MIF	Miners' International Federation
NKV	Nederlands Katholiek Vakverbond (Netherlands Catholic Trade Union Federation)
NVV	Nederlands Verbond van Vakverenigingen (Netherlands Federation of Trade Unions)
OATUU	Organization of African Trade Union Unity
ÖGB	Österreichischer Gewerkschaftsbund (Austrian Federation of Trade Unions)
ORIT	Interamerican Regional Organization of Workers (ICFTU)
PAFL	Pan-American Federation of Labor
PAWC	Pan-African Workers Congress (WCL)
PSI	Public Services International
PTTI	Postal, Telegraph and Telephone International
RILU	Red International of Labor Unions
TUAC-OECD	Trade Union Advisory Committee to the Organization for Economic Cooperation and Development
TUC	Trades Union Congress (Great Britain)
TUI	Trade Union International (WFTU)
UGTAN	Union Générale des Travailleurs d'Afrique Noire (General Union of Workers of Black Africa)
UIL	Unione Italiana del Lavoro (Italian Union of Labor)
WCL	World Confederation of Labor
WFTU	World Federation of Trade Unions

Tables

Chapter I. The Historical Background to 1919

1. Although the idea of an international association of working people emerged in hazy image already in the 1830s, a concrete organizational form did not develop until some thirty years later. As usual in these matters, it came about as a result of several coinciding events among which it would be difficult to identify the decisive one.

2. There was, above all, the enormous progress in technology and science which greatly facilitated travel and communications, even among workers and organizations appealing for working class support. On the occasion of the International Exhibition in London in 1862, the French government, hoping to pacify its own restless working class by bringing it in contact with the moderate elements of New Model Unionism in Britain, financed a trip by several hundred elected worker delegates to visit the Exhibition. Some of the French visitors were sought out by the leaders of the newly established London Trades Council whose unfortunate experience with imported continental strikebreakers in labour conflicts, notably in the London building industry, had persuaded them of the importance of establishing protective links with workers on the continent. In the following year (1863) political developments on the continent, notably those involving the struggle for Polish independence against Russian rule, led British and French workers on several occasions to express support for the insurgents, and at a further meeting in London in July 1863, held in conjunction with the Polish cause, British and French representatives reached agreement in principle on the formation of an international labour organization.

A. The First International (1864–1876)

3. To forward the agreed objective the British trade unions formally affirmed their belief in the need for an international labour body by sending an 'address to the workingmen of France'. It had been drafted by George Odger who was then secretary of the London Trades Council, and it dealt with foreign affairs (notably the Polish question), social reform, and the importance of strengthened trade union rights. The French prepared an equally formal reply which expressed concern over the continuing concentration of capital and stressed the goal of institutionalizing international labour solidarity by means of an Association. Transmission of the French reply was entrusted to a delegation for whose proper reception a meeting was arranged on 28 September 1864, at St.

Martin's Hall in London. So as to ensure a desirable international atmosphere, the hosts – a group of London trade unions – invited a number of political refugees living in exile in London, Karl Marx among them, to attend. That meeting voted to establish an International Working Men's Association with headquarters in London and with branches in other European capitals. It decided to entrust the draft of a programme and constitution to a committee of mixed nationalities and political views, and the committee in turn delegated its assignment to Karl Marx. His adroitness as a draftsman produced an 'Address to the Working Classes' (or 'Inaugural Address') to whose deliberately moderate and in places ambiguous terms the adherents of widely disparate political views could readily subscribe.

4. In the preamble to the statutes of the International Working Men's Association – or the First International as it would later be known – Marx formulated the principles of the organization in terms that pointed to the economic emancipation of the working class as the overriding goal to which every political movement was to be subordinated as a means. It may well be that he chose this formulation in order to recognize the primary trade union character of the principal affiliates of the organization, the British trade unions, although there was no explicit mention of trade unions. The point was underlined by another clause of the preamble which attributed all servitude, social misery, mental degradation and political dependence to the economic subjection of the working man. The statutes proper envisaged an organization whose principal task it would be to coordinate the activities of its affiliated national sections toward the achievement of the complete emancipation of the working classes. An annual Congress was designated as the highest authority of the International, and provision was made for the election by the Congress of a General Council. The General Council, in turn, was to select the officers and to act as a coordinating agency between the several national and local affiliates. The final version of the statutes was adopted only in 1871, but in provisional form they were already approved at the meeting of the First Congress in Geneva in 1866.

5. It is difficult to specify the size of the Association at various points of its existence. There probably were never more than a thousand members in Germany, perhaps a few thousand in Italy, and not many more in the United States. More sizable affiliations were secured in Britain and claimed for France and Spain. Affiliates also existed in Belgium, Switzerland, and other countries. The perennial financial troubles of the organization indicate that the concept of membership did not necessarily have a financial meaning.

6. The First International was neither a federation of national organizations nor a body based on trade unions. It was made up, instead, of a mixture of individual members, who joined branches and sections in each country, as well as of collectively affiliated trade unions, notably those from Britain. Where they existed, national sections were supposed to link together the local branches whose membership often consisted more of members of the middle classes, professionals, and intellectuals than manual workers. In fact, middle class membership had been among the first of many controversial issues; the French had lost that argument.

7. The influence of the First International on the character and growth of European working class organizations was assessed by G. D. H. Cole in his *History of Socialist Thought* in these terms:

'The International was launched at a moment when Europe was from end to end in a condition of acute disquiet, and it developed during the next few years in an environment of spreading wars and revolutions. In general, up to the outbreak of the Franco-Prussian War of 1870, these conditions favoured its growth; and they certainly increased its stature in the eyes of its enemies, who were very ready to attribute to it every manifestation of popular unrest. The International also got the credit – or the blame – for the great increase in strikes, which was in fact largely the outcome of the economic crisis of 1866–7 and of the ensuing revival. It is probable that the existence of the International was a factor in stimulating the rapid growth of Trade Unionism in a number of countries during these years; but to a considerable extent this growth would have occurred without it, as a natural reaction to the prevailing economic conditions. Certainly the course of Trade Union development in both Great Britain and France, and also in Belgium, can be explained without much reference to the International; and in Germany the International had almost no influence on the course of events. In Spain, the great development of working-class organisation took place mainly in its name, but quite independently of any direction from the General Council in London; and in Italy the movement was influenced much more by Bakunin than by Marx or the General Council, and never owed more than the barest allegiance to the I.W.M.A. It is indeed difficult to point to any country in which the International as an organisation really supplied the main driving force. For the most part, the working-class movement in each country went its own way, whether or not it acted mainly in the International's name. The International gave some help in strikes, both by collecting money and by preventing the transport of strike-breakers across national frontiers; but beyond this it could do little to guide the course of events. It was able to make a great deal of stir, and to arouse large fears in the minds of its opponents, as well as large hopes among its supporters. But its real power was always narrowly limited; and the foundations of what power it had ever possessed had been undermined well before the doctrinal disputes within it had reached their head.'

8. Almost from the very beginning there were internal disagreements, mostly over ideology and principles. In the initial years the confrontations at annual congresses (Geneva 1866, Lausanne 1867, Brussels 1868, and Basel 1869) usually pitted the followers of Marx against the adherents of Proudhon. Towards the end of the decade the Proudhonists passed from the stage, and by 1871 their position as the chief adversaries of Marx was occupied by Michel Bakunin and his anarchist followers. The disagreements encompassed both philosophical and strategic issues and had a personal dimension as well.

Against Marx's intermediate aim of the political conquest of the state by disciplined and centrally led or at least well coordinated battalions of the working class Bakunin pressed the destruction of the state and all its institutions as inherently oppressive forms of social organization. Freedom, autonomy, and decentralization were the indispensable elements in Bakunin's libertarian worldview, and unlike Marx he was not prepared to enter even temporarily into tactical compromises with other social movements, most certainly not those of a bourgeois character.

9. Until the outbreak of the Franco-Prussian War of 1870–71 the International had steadily expanded its membership and strengthened its reputation. The war, however, marked a change, notably because of the rise of the Paris Commune in 1871 to which the International, after first warning French workers not to engage in acts of desperation, subsequently extended its full support. The address on the 'Civil War in France', which Marx read to the General Council shortly after the collapse of the Commune, defended and praised the Commune as a spontaneously conceived but nevertheless correct form of a revolutionary working class government. The address was published under the International's imprimatur and attracted a barrage of public criticism. Two British trade union leaders resigned almost at once from the General Council, and it is likely that the trade union affiliates, especially in Great Britain, began to reconsider their collective affiliation.

10. The dispute between Marx and Bakunin came to a head at the Congress of the Hague in 1872, the first one to be held after the 1869 meeting in Basel. Marx, whose hold on the organization had become precarious, succeeded in mustering a majority of the delegates for his three principal objectives – strengthening the powers of the General Council, expelling Bakunin, and removing the headquarters of the International from London to New York where it might be more easily defended against take-over attempts. But it was a pyrrhic victory, for once shifted to New York, the organization lost touch with the European labour movements. In Julius Braunthal's view 'the crisis of the Internationale was basically a crisis associated with the growth of the European labour movement. As the movement in the several countries became stronger, it regarded the leading role of the General Council as a burdensome encroachment on its autonomy. Marx viewed the International as the super-party of the working classes of all countries and the General Council as the party's head. But each one of the individual labour movements rather considered itself as an independent party, eager to develop its own ideology and to determine its own policies.'

11. From its New York headquarters the General Council convened a congress to be held in Geneva in 1873 (it would have been the sixth) but almost all the delegates were local people, and no General Council members attended. There was now nothing left except to dissolve the body. The formal act occurred at a final meeting of the General Council in Philadelphia in 1876.

B. The Second International (1889–1914)

12. During the 1870s and even more so during the 1880s, socialist parties and trade unions in most European countries made impressive headway. In some countries, such as Germany, they successfully surmounted severe legal obstacles to their advancement. Their growth and rising power laid the basis for a revival of efforts to forge once more an organization that could effectively represent the sentiments of international labour solidarity which were professed by working class organizations. In the ensuing efforts the leadership role was assumed for the most part by the three foremost European countries – France, Great Britain and Germany. Their labour and socialist movements were the largest and the most influential ones.

13. The initial attempts to rebuild an international alliance occurred under French auspices. Moderate French socialists, often referred to as Possibilists because their aims emphasized objectives considered attainable in society as constituted, convened two international labour congresses that met in Paris in 1883 and again in 1886. The Marxist socialists of France (Guesdists) stayed away, but representatives from the British Trades Union Congress (TUC), the loosely organized central body of British trade unionism, were in attendance.

14. Consonant with the moderate views of most participants, the congresses debated such issues as the need for improved working conditions and shorter hours in industry. No far reaching substantive or organizational results were reached, but at French suggestion the British TUC agreed to sponsor another international congress in London in 1888. From this gathering the organizers – the Parliamentary Committee of the TUC – carefully excluded socialist (Marxist) party representatives, but a few nevertheless squeezed in with the help of trade union accreditations. Obtaining trade union credentials was not an unusual feat for a socialist party leader since in most European countries the organizational distinction between party and union was at that time still blurred.

15. The main substantive item on the agenda in London was again an industrial issue, the call for a legally mandated eight-hour day, but there was also strong sentiment for moving toward a permanent international labour body. In response the delegates took the decision to convene a founding congress the following year, 1889, in Paris.

16. The exclusion of Marxist socialists from the London meeting and their expectation of being excluded from the forthcoming Paris meeting led the German and French Marxist socialist parties to issue a call for their own socialist congress. It, too, was to meet in Paris and surely not just by coincidence at exactly the same time. To compound the confusion, the French Possibilists who at the London congress had undertaken to organize the meeting of the moderates and trade unionists did not adhere to the agreement but instead distributed their invitations more widely than planned. Thus two socialist congresses met in Paris in July 1889, one arranged by the French Possibilists, the other by their Marxist rivals. A few delegates managed to attend both congresses. The moderates had about 600 delegates in attendance, the Marxists some 400. In both halls the French hosts far outnumbered all the others. Efforts to unite the two congresses ended in complete failure.

17. The Marxist meeting was the more distinguished one. It included most of the best known leaders of the European Marxist socialist parties and their allied trade union movements. Especially strong was the German delegation. It is, therefore, this meeting that has come to be regarded as the beginning of a new Socialist International (soon known as the Second International).

18. The main item on the official agenda of both meetings was virtually identical: the international promotion of labour legislation, with urgent reference to instituting the eight-hour day. The original impetus for an international campaign to achieve the eight-hour day had come from the American Federation of Labor, and following its initiative the socialist delegates in Paris decided to proclaim 1 May 1890, as an occasion for international demonstrations on behalf of labour's causes and for celebrating the solidarity of the international labour movement.

19. No permanent international machinery emerged from Paris. That was to come later. But the idea was now widely accepted that international socialist congresses were a useful institution, and from this time on until the outbreak of World War I they were held regularly at intervals of three to four years: Brussels 1891; Zurich 1893, London 1896, Paris again in 1900, Amsterdam 1904, Stuttgart 1907, and Copenhagen 1910. There was a special congress in Basel in 1912, and there should have been another regular congress in Vienna in October 1914, but the war prevented it.

20. An issue disposed of relatively early was the relationship of socialists to the anarchist movement which had strong adherents in the Mediterranean countries, though by no means confined to that area. Although there was from the very beginning overwhelming opposition to anarchist participation, the question had to be resolved in such a way that bona fide trade unionists, whose presence was welcomed, would not be excluded by rules aimed at anarchists and anarcho-syndicalists with trade union credentials. By the time of the London congress (1896) an acceptable formulation had been found to exclude anarchists and other opponents of parliamentary action, but the definitive rules which barred the anti-parliamentarians yet kept socialist trade unions within the fold were not adopted until the Paris congress in 1900.

21. By 1900, too, the continuity of the international socialist movement was firmly enough established to warrant the formation of a permanent secretariat. Its seat was to be in Brussels, the capital of a neutral country whose socialist party was neither so large nor so ambitious as to aspire to a hegemonic role in the organization. Under the statutes adopted at the Paris meeting in 1900 the Second International was composed of socialist parties and of those trade unions that were committed to political action through legislative and parliamentary channels. The governing body was designated as the International Socialist Bureau, made up of two members from each affiliated party. The powers of the Bureau were limited. It could not commit the national parties to any particular course of action. Nevertheless, in time the Bureau acquired a moral and intellectual authority that enabled it to exert a certain amount of influence on socialist party policies at national and international levels. Thus it helped to unify the fragmented movement in France, grappled with the question of socialist participation in bourgeois governments, beat back challenges to Marxist orthodoxy by the adherents of revisionism and reformism (but in subtle ways gradually adapted to the new realism), fought over the use of the general strike as a means for achieving or at least bringing closer the ultimate social revolution, and agonized over the proper position to take in the event a general war threatened to break out. Most of the time the leading role was taken by the German Social Democratic Party whose numbers, discipline, achievements, and contributions to socialist thought far eclipsed the role of other parties. The foremost rivals of the Germans were the French, but their influence suffered from internecine conflicts and deplorable organizational shortcomings.

22. The Second International also claimed to speak on behalf of trade unions. It was a reasonable claim, at least in the initial ten to fifteen years, for in most countries the major trade union organizations were connected with the socialist parties in close alliance, even if subordinate to the parties both in practice and in doctrine.

23. As to practice, several union movements owed their very existence to party-initiated organizing efforts, and the central body of the party often served simultaneously as the central organ for the unions. Moreover, most union leaders were active members of the socialist party and generally prepared to accept its discipline, at least in the Northern European countries.

24. As to doctrine, the party was regarded as the guiding political force of the working class. Therefore, it was the party that exercised responsibility for deciding all major issues of theory and strategy arising in the class struggle and in the pursuit of the ultimate goal – the establishment of a socialist society. After some initial hesitation the unions, too, were recognized as an important element in the struggle. They were to be schools of socialism and organs for recruiting workers into the movement. The top leaders of the unions were important party figures and occupied seats on party executives, though they rarely penetrated to the very front ranks of party leadership. But the economic and industrial aims of the unions, while acknowledged as important in their own right, were deemed to be subordinate to the party's broader political and social objectives. It followed logically that the unions' day-by-day efforts to extract material improvements from resisting employers and to secure protective labour legislation from hostile or indifferent governments were of only secondary importance by comparison with the far-reaching political aims of the socialist party. In point of fact, union dealings with employers tended to evoke no little suspicion among the left wing of the socialist parties because such rapprochements seemed to verge on class collaboration and to turn the attention of the masses away from revolutionary goals.

25. An important exception to this somewhat schematic description was the relationship between the trade unions and political groups in Britain. There the trade unions had so far preceded the formation of socialist bodies and had already so firmly established themselves in society and industry, that the Labour party, when it emerged, did so as the instrument of the unions instead of the other way around. As a result the general character of the labour movement in Britain was less determined by ideology than the continental movements and correspondingly more pragmatic in its goals and means.

26. In a certain sense, however, developments on the continent, too, soon tended to move toward more pragmatism. Initially, as noted, the parties had often been the founders and at least at first the financial supporters of the unions. But within hardly more than a decade the strength of the unions began, first to rival, and then to surpass that of the parties. In all European countries caught up in the vast industrialization process during the two or three decades before 1914, the membership, financial resources, and striking power of the unions developed more rapidly than similar indicators in the socialist parties. It was thus unavoidable that many newcomers to the unions joined not because of newly discovered socialist convictions but because they sought to protect their jobs, improve their pay, and secure better conditions of work through collective demands put before employers. The resulting ideological dilution of the unions and the increased strength which rapid growth conferred on them resulted in a fundamental shift of party–union relations in almost every country. Increasingly the unions demanded the right to make their own decision free of party interference in all questions involving their relations with employers, while at the same time they became ever more reluctant to put their organizations at the disposal of the parties for political purposes.

27. In fact, through the spread of collective bargaining, the conclusion of agreements, the establishment of conciliation and arbitration systems, and of course also due to gradual changes in employer attitudes, the unions were acquiring vested interests in the preservation of the existing systems of industrial relations. At the very least they became increasingly hesitant to let ideological issues determine their attitudes toward employers and steadily more intolerant of outside intervention in their own affairs, even from a fraternal socialist party. In the resulting conflicts over proper party–union relations the left insisted on party supremacy, the right, which included the unions, espoused equality, and the centre tried to bridge the gap through conciliation and reformulations of inherited doctrine.

28. With their increasing resources and self-confidence the unions proved to be the stronger side. In most countries before the turn of the century, and in a few others shortly thereafter, the unions established their own central federations, thus ending their institutional dependence on – and their hierarchical subordination to – the central executives of the parties. As a result the socialist and labour movements acquired two central bodies – one for the party and another for the unions. Often they agreed from the very start on reciprocal representation on their executive bodies and on an exchange of fraternal delegates at their congresses.

29. The rise of powerful unions entailed not only far-reaching consequences for domestic union–party relations but also resulted in structural modifications at international level. Two kinds of development need to be distinguished: the formation of international bodies for unions in individual trades and industries and the establishment of an international organization for national trade union centres.

C. International Trade Secretariats

30. The first individual unions to form their own internationals were organizations operating in closely related trades and industries. Later known, collectively, as International Trade Secretariats, they sought to unite in loose associations the national unions of boot and shoe workers (1889), miners (1890), printers (1893), clothing workers (1893), metal workers (1893), textile workers (1894), transport workers (1897), and many other groups including even such specialized crafts as hatters (1900), stone workers (1903), diamond workers (1905), pottery workers (1905), and hairdressers (1907).

31. These combinations of unions were based on the presumed existence of an international community of interests, a set of shared problems and experiences, and an expectation of increased strength through mutual help. The congresses of the Second International usually served as the initial meeting grounds where organizational ties were established and agreements reached on structure, finances, and staffing. By 1914 there were almost 30 International Trade Secretariats, most of them with headquarters in Germany.

32. Since most of their national affiliates were part of the socialist movement in their own countries, the Secretariats usually professed long-term aims which identified them as part of the international socialist movement. For example, they supported the nationalization of the means of production and the replacement of the capitalist system by socialism. But in practice they concentrated their attention on more practical objectives, such as an exchange of information on wages and working conditions, prevention of international strikebreaking efforts by employers, mutual recognition of union membership cards, reciprocal financial assistance in times of severe industrial conflict, and the organization of employment information for journeymen who wanted to work and travel abroad before settling down to a steady job at home. This was unspectacular work, and there was usually not enough of it to keep even a single secretary employed full-time. But it was useful work, nevertheless, especially in those industries, like merchant shipping, whose international character clearly required some form of international exchange of information.

D. International Secretariat of Trade Union Centres (1901–1913)

33. It took somewhat longer for the second type of international trade union organization, one based on national trade union centres, to be established. The problem was the competence of the Second International whose congresses dealt not only with political issues but covered the full range of working class interests, including matters of primary concern to trade unions. Thus, the agenda of the first few congresses included the eight-hour day, child labour, night work for women, industrial health and safety and similar items. Of course, the congresses included representatives of parties and trade unions, including British trade unions which did not subscribe to the socialist aims of the Second International.

34. The German union leaders, with close relations to the powerful German Social Democratic party, were most opposed to the creation of an international trade union body that might duplicate the jurisdiction of the Second International, but eventually they were persuaded that it might be useful for national trade union centres (at that time also referred to as national secretariats) to meet from time to time separately from the parties for an exchange of views and experiences of a strictly trade union character. The first meeting of this kind took place in 1901 when national trade union officials from Germany, Belgium, France, Finland and Great Britain accepted an invitation to attend a conference of Scandinavian trade unions in Copenhagen.

35. There it was agreed to hold such meetings periodically in conjunction with a national trade union congress, and a second conference convened the following year (1902) in Stuttgart. The Germans offered to act as a central secretariat, or International Centre, and to pay all costs for the coming year.

36. At the next congress in Dublin in 1903 responsibility for continued administration was entrusted to an international secretary, the German trade union leader Carl Legien. To meet rising costs, a decision was taken to impose an affiliation fee of sixpence, or 50 pfennig, per 1,000 members.

37. Three other decisions taken in Dublin deserve notice. First, it was provided that only national centres could be represented at future meetings, not individual unions. This rule was intended to protect the international body from becoming involved in internal national disputes and to ensure uniformity of representation. Second, only delegates living in the country whose trade union centre they represented could attend. The idea was to bar political refugees with unverifiable credentials. Finally, biennial meetings were henceforth to take the place of annual meetings.

38. Before the next conference met in Amsterdam in 1905, Legien became involved in a major controversy with the French affiliate, the Confédération Générale de Travail (CGT). The CGT, many of whose leaders were at the time strongly under the influence of syndicalist ideology, wanted to add the general strike, anti-militarism, and the eight-hour day to the agenda. Legien, a social democrat, objected on the grounds that at least the first two items did not properly belong to the work of the conference. The French protested, Legien consulted his affiliates, their replies mostly supported him, and the CGT decided not to be represented in Amsterdam.

39. The Amsterdam conference in 1905 confirmed Legien's conception of the organization's limits. By majority vote it decided to exclude 'all theoretical questions and questions affecting tendencies and tactics'. It also accepted Legien's formulation of its tasks as consisting of promoting closer ties between unions in all countries, collecting trade union statistics, and providing mutual support in times of conflict. The statement of tasks was not essentially different from the provisions which Marx had included in the draft statutes of the First International a generation earlier.

40. When the International Secretariat met in Christiania (Oslo) in 1907, it reaffirmed the definition of its tasks as expressed in Amsterdam two years earlier. The French again remained away in protest against the majority's refusal to take up the general strike and anti-militarism. Among substantive issues the meeting considered a report on the relationship between unemployment and hours of work, the need for improved ways of transferring trade union membership for migrant and emigrant workers, and the problem of international strikebreaking. It also increased the dues to one shilling and sixpence.

41. Ever since it had first begun to hold meetings the International Secretariat had consisted overwhelmingly of socialist trade union federations in Western and Central Europe. On the right wing the British membership was occupied by the obscure General Federation of Trade Unions rather than the much larger but also much more loosely organized Trades Union Congress. (The latter effectively replaced the GFTU only after World War I.) At the left stood the French CGT. The major outsider among the still limited number of industrialized countries was the United States where the principal labour movement, the American Federation of Labor, had rejected socialism as its ideology. That had not kept the International Secretariat from repeatedly inviting the AFL into membership. But until 1909 the AFL had politely refused all invitations.

42. It was in Paris in 1909 that the AFL was for the first time represented at a conference of the International Secretariat. AFL President Samuel Gompers emphasized that he was present only as a fraternal delegate without a mandate to bind his organization, but he indicated that if the Secretariat saw fit to adopt a name conveying more meaning to American workers than the term secretariat – such as International Federation of Labor – and if the Federation could guarantee the autonomy of its member organizations, an AFL affiliation would probably follow.

43. No formal action was taken on either proposal. But there seem to have been informal reassurances, for in 1910 the AFL became an affiliated organization. Its membership was promptly challenged. The Industrial Workers of the World sent an envoy to the next meeting in Budapest (1911) to protest against the admission of the AFL on the ground that the AFL was an organization for class collaboration rather than for the defence of workers' interests against employers. After considerable discussion the protest was rejected. Delegates were not obliged, so the majority held, to justify the tactics of their organization or their own political views. Concurrently the IWW's own application for affiliation was rejected under the rule adopted earlier that only one national centre from one country could belong. Interestingly, the conference also turned down a bid to affiliate by the Canadian Federation of Labor because the AFL asserted with success that the Canadian labour unions were an integral part of its own organization.

44. The last conference before the war met in Zurich in 1913. For the first time fraternal delegates from the International Trade Secretariats were present, a practice that was to be continued after the war. The delegates took a number of decisions which implied strong confidence in the permanence of their bonds. For one thing they adopted unanimously an AFL proposal to change the name of the organization to the International Federation of Trade Unions (IFTU). Second, they adopted a new administrative structure with a president, Carl Legien, at the head and a full-time secretary. Third, they decided to approve a trilingual newsletter that had begun to appear earlier in the year. Fourth, they voted to raise the dues from 1½ to 4 German Marks. Finally, they decided to accept the AFL's invitation to hold their next conference in San Francisco in 1915. That meeting was, of course, never held. Nor has any similar meeting subsequently been held in the United States.

E. International Federation of Trade Unions (1913–1919)

45. By 1913 the membership of the IFTU had risen to about 7.5 million, distributed among approximately 20 organizations. The largest affiliates were from Germany, the United States, and Great Britain, with France and Austria also well represented, but the German labour federation was preeminent in the IFTU, just as German unions stood first in most of the International Trade Secretariats.

46. German leadership was based on organizational and ideological foundations. Socialist trade unionism in Germany was an exceedingly well organized

Membership of International Federation of Trade Unions, 1904–1913

Year	Number of affiliated national centers	Membership (approximately)
1904	14	2,500,000
1905	14	3,000,000
1906	15	3,500,000
1907	17	4,000,000
1908	18	4,250,000
1909	20	5,800,000
1910	20	6,000,000
1911	19	7,000,000
1912	19	7,400,000
1913	19	7,700,000

and disciplined movement by comparison with most other countries. And in the realm of socialist thought the German labour movement was acknowledged to be foremost by its sister movements in Austria, the Scandinavian countries, Belgium, the Netherlands, Switzerland, and elsewhere. Revolutionary syndicalism as an alternative collectivist doctrine was significant among IFTU affiliates only in France, Italy, and Spain, while trade unionism in a predominantly non-ideological sense was prevalent only in Great Britain and the United States.

47. Before the war, the main practical work of the IFTU consisted of the collection and dissemination of information useful to its members and of strike aid. The information included data on union membership, labour disputes, labour legislation, and similar items. Strike aid consisted not only of collections on behalf of unions involved in major disputes but also of efforts to prevent the use of strikebreakers across national borders.

48. The outbreak of World War I severely disrupted international trade union organizations. The principal socialist and labour movements in the warring countries supported their governments without serious reservations. As the war mounted in intensity the barriers between national movements rose. In Berlin the headquarters of the IFTU continued to maintain relations with trade unions in neutral countries, but Legien's attempt to maintain contacts with the allies through the neutral Dutch affiliate failed when the French unions established their own International Correspondence Bureau in Paris. In 1916 it organized an Inter-Allied Trade Union Conference in Leeds attended by French, British, Belgian, and Italian delegates. This conference issued a programme of detailed social demands that was intended for incorporation in the peace treaty.

49. The German reply to the Leeds meeting was a call for a trade union conference to gather in Stockholm in June 1917. It was intended to be inclusive but was attended only by unions from the Central Powers and several neutral countries. In the hope of obtaining a more representative meeting the conferees asked the Swiss to call another conference which met in Bern in October 1917. However, no representatives from the Allied countries attended. The programme of social demands adopted in Bern corresponded in many respects to the demands agreed to at the Leeds conference.

50. After the Armistice the first meeting of trade union delegates from the opposing sides and from neutral countries occurred at a hastily arranged conference in Bern in February 1919. At this second Bern conference a consolidated programme of labour demands was adopted which particularly envisaged the adoption of a comprehensive set of international labour laws. The conference also decided to proceed with the reconstitution of the International Federation of Trade Unions.

Chapter II. The Historical Background 1919–1939

A. Reconstitution and Division (1919–1923)

51. The social programme agreed upon at the second Bern conference was placed before the Commission on International Labour Legislation constituted by the Allied Powers at the Versailles Peace Conference in order to review labour's conception of the international order in the postwar period. The final report of this commission, chaired by Samuel Gompers of the AFL, became Part XIII of the Versailles Peace Treaty. It provided for the establishment of a permanent tripartite institution, the International Labour Organization (ILO), which was empowered to formulate and promulgate standards of international social policy through the adoption of international conventions and recommendations. (A separate volume of this Encyclopaedia is devoted to the International Labour Organization.)

52. The creation of the ILO became a major item of discussion at the international trade union congress in Amsterdam in July–August 1919 which had been called to reconstruct the International Federation of Trade Unions. The congress was attended by national federations from 14 countries in Europe and North America, representing a total of almost 17 million members. The figure is indicative of the increase in unionization that occurred during and immediately after the war in almost every industrialized country.

53. The Amsterdam meeting adopted a new IFTU constitution. It provided for the autonomy of all affiliates, a rule that only one organization could be affiliated from any one country, and a proportional system of voting at IFTU congresses. The governing hierarchy was to consist of a biennial congress and an elected Management Committee. As one of the after effects of the war, the seat of the secretariat was shifted from Berlin to neutral Amsterdam, and two trade union officials of Dutch nationality – Jan Oudegeest and Edo Fimmen – were appointed as secretaries.

54. Aside from a conflict over a demand for a German trade union declaration of war guilt, which the Germans reluctantly conceded, serious differences at the Amsterdam congress arose mostly between the European and the American delegations. The latter objected to several decisions, including a resolution critical of the League of Nations, another resolution that constituted an endorsement of socialism, a rule providing that all resolutions adopted by majority vote would be binding on affiliates (thus seemingly nullifying the constitutionally guaranteed autonomy of all affiliates), and an affiliation fee of $4.50 per 1,000 members which not only the Americans but also the British deemed excessive. Because of all these reservations the AFL delegates did not commit themselves to join the reconstituted IFTU, and indeed subsequently the AFL decided not to resume membership in the IFTU. There followed a protracted series of negotiations to resolve outstanding differences, but it was not until 1937 that the AFL returned. During the first half of this period of separation the AFL turned its attention to Latin America where in 1918 it had joined with the Mexican trade union federation CROM in creating a Pan-American Federation of Labor (PAFL). AFL interest in its activities declined after the death of Samuel Gompers in 1924, and during the 1930s the PAFL ceased to function.

55. The disruptions caused by the war affected the socialist parties even more severely than the trade unions, and consequently it took them longer than the unions to reestablish their international institutions in effective form. Moreover, the splits which occurred in almost every country between socialists and communists extended also to the international level where new communist-led political organizations (the Third International or Comintern) and trade union organization (the Red International or Labour Unions or Profintern) arose in fierce competition with already existing socialist organizations.

56. The Second International sought to reconstruct its shattered ranks at conferences in Berne in 1919 and Geneva in 1920 but without substantial success. A considerable number of left wing socialist parties, many of whom had split off during the war from the main socialist parties in various countries, decided to form their own international organization in 1921 under the name of the International Working Union of Socialist Parties, also known as the Vienna Union or the Two-and-a-Half International because ideologically it seemed to stand about half way between the socialist and communist internationals. After the failure of an attempt in 1922 in Berlin to create a united and all-inclusive International out of the three competing blocs, the Second International and the Vienna Union succeeded in uniting their own forces in 1923 at a congress in Hamburg. The name chosen for their organization at this meeting was the Labour and Socialist International (LSI), though ideologically the new body was really a continuation of the Second International. Among its declared objectives was the maintenance of a close relationship with the International Federation of Trade Unions.

57. By 1923, therefore, the postwar structure of international labour movements had become solidified once again but it was now far more complex and divided than before the war. For alongside the separate socialist internationals of political parties and trade unions there also existed henceforth a set of parallel communist internationals and, as we shall note below, a separate trade union international also for Christian labour organizations.

B. Red International Labour Unions (1921–1943)

58. It was the Bolshevik revolution in Russia in 1917 that led to a major realignment of the political and trade union groupings in the international labour movement. At a March 1919 conference in Moscow, called by the Communist party of the USSR, a new political international was established under Russian leadership which called itself the Communist International (Comintern) or Third International. Its aim was to carry the revolution into the capitalist camp.

59. From the very outset the Comintern adopted a sharply antagonistic position toward non-Communist working class organizations, especially those inspired by social democracy, accusing them of having surrendered their proletarian revolutionary heritage to a futile parliamentarianism and class collaboration. It called on workers everywhere to abandon the socialist parties and trade unions and to join the newly forming Communist organizations as the only genuine representatives of working class interests. Consistent with their claim to exclusive leadership of the working class, the Bolsheviks refused an invitation to attend the Amsterdam trade union conference in 1919 and to make common cause with social democratic political and trade union groups.

60. Initially the Bolshevik leadership in Russia was undecided about establishing a separate Communist trade union international alongside the Comintern, the alternative being to treat the Third International as both a political and a trade union grouping. In the early part of 1920 the Russian trade unions actually resolved to join the Comintern as their international organization and to urge unions in other countries to follow them, but soon thereafter Lenin decided that there ought to be a separate Communist-directed trade union international after all. In line with that decision an inaugural congress of the Red International of Labour Unions (Profintern) was held in Moscow in 1921 with delegates present from 38 countries. Many of the non-Russian delegates represented minority groups in their own national trade union movements.

61. The initial programme of the RILU expressed unrelenting hostility toward the IFTU and its affiliates but did not urge RILU affiliates to split from or abandon their national labour movements. Instead, Communist cadres and their adherents in the social-democratic unions were urged to redouble their activity within the existing organizations for the purpose of ultimately taking them over. The RILU founding congress also endorsed the transformation of craft unions into industrial unions and the establishment of works councils on a massive scale as incipient revolutionary bodies on the model of the soviets in prerevolutionary Russia.

62. The competitive situation created by the establishment of the RILU became a preeminent factor in the structure of international trade unionism throughout much of the interwar period. Although the IFTU was at all times the more representative and clearly the more experienced organization, its Communist rival was often able to exercise the initiative as the more aggressive and monolithic organization. Its decisions on strategy and tactics usually set the tone for the relationship with the IFTU, the International Trade Secretariats, and individual IFTU affiliates, and there can be little doubt that throughout much of the 1920s the RILU considered itself to be in the ascendancy, while regarding the IFTU as facing inexorable decline and eventual collapse.

63. For most of the 1920s, the RILU continued to follow its initial policy of ostensibly striving for 'international trade union unity' and, in individual countries, of forming a 'united front' with socialist and other organizations as far as possible. In this endeavour the Soviet trade unions, under the direction of the centralized All Union Central Council of Trade Unions (AUCCTU), played a particularly important role because they were by far the most important constituent bloc in the RILU. In 1924 the AUCCTU even succeeded in obtaining the agreement of the British TUC to the formation of an Anglo-Russian Committee to promote international trade union unity. For about two years this committee played a significant role in international trade union affairs. In particular it served the TUC and notably some of its left wing leaders as an instrument to try to bring about a rapprochement between the socialist and Communist wings of the international trade union movement. In pursuit of this objective the TUC pressed strongly for IFTU acceptance of affiliation by the AUCCTU on terms repeatedly characterized by the IFTU as unacceptable. The key obstacle to the admission of the AUCCTU was Russian insistence on the need for negotiating changes in existing IFTU rules before the Russians would enter the organization, while for its part the IFTU insisted that the Russian unions had to declare their independence from the Communist party and government before being allowed to join. The TUC effort failed, but the Anglo-Russian Committee constituted for some time a tenuous link between the two international groupings. The British leadership dissolved the Committee in 1927 after experiencing considerable disillusionment over its dealings with the AUCCTU, especially in connection with the general strike of 1926 and AUCCTU activities which the TUC regarded as gross interference in its internal affairs.

64. Membership figures for the RILU during the 1920s are difficult to assess because of its peculiar mix of affiliates, the unstable character of their affiliation, and the unverifiability of the membership claims. Among its member organizations the RILU included not only national majority and minority centres, such as at various times those in the Soviet Union, China, Australia, France, Bulgaria, Czechoslovakia, Norway and Finland, but also assorted pressure groups, action committees, leagues of individual workers, sympathizers, and other varied categories. It has been estimated that the RILU began with perhaps 8 million members in 1921 and that it reached a high point for the decade in 1927 with perhaps 12 million. The Russian affiliate all by itself, the AUCCTU, always accounted for at least two-thirds of total RILU membership.

65. Just as the Russian trade unions furnished the bulk of the RILU membership, so they or the Soviet Communist party or government also provided virtually all the requisite financial support and the top administrative echelons. Its highest governing organ was the congress which elected a central council composed of over one hundred members. The council, in turn, chose an Executive Bureau of 14 members drawn from several affiliates, but from the very beginning the RILU functioned under the general guidance of the Comintern and more particularly the Communist party leadership of the USSR. Day-to-day administration was in the hands of Alexander Lozovsky, the general secretary, who was also a member of the Central Committee of the Communist party of the USSR.

66. In about 1928 the Communists' long standing 'united front' policy of tactical but vigilant and adversary cooperation with socialist groups was superseded by a major switch to a policy of outright confrontation. It was accompanied by an equally sharp turn in Soviet domestic policies. The theory underlying the new position was that social democracy had revealed itself to an ever-increasing extent as a form of social fascism which only served the bourgeoisie as an instrument for the political and economic oppression of the masses. Communist trade unions were now instructed to fight openly against their social democratic rivals, rather than to seek to undermine them from within, and wherever possible to establish dual unions under their own control.

67. The new course lasted, however, for only a few years. The victory of National Socialism in Germany in 1933 and the acute danger of its spread to other European countries led the Soviet Union in 1934–35 to revise its external policies and to aim for closer relations with the Western democratic countries. This change in policy extended equally to the attitudes that national Communist parties and trade unions were henceforth expected to adopt toward the political parties of the centre and the left and toward social democratic trade unions. The period of cooperation which ensued is generally referred to as the Popular Front.

68. At international level the remarkable change had fatal consequences for the RILU. In one of its last official acts the RILU in 1935 proposed to the IFTU a joint conference to seek ways of establishing international trade union unity. Rejection of the proposal coincided with the effective termination of RILU activities. Though the organization was not yet formally dissolved, it became inoperative. Lozovsky was relieved of his responsibilities as RILU secretary-general and shifted to an administrative position in the USSR State Publishing House. The formal act of dissolution occurred in 1943, parallel with the end of the Third International.

C. International Federation of Trade Unions (1919–1939)

69. For the IFTU the interwar period presented a succession of political problems of such overriding importance that they could not be set aside as irrelevant to the concerns of an essentially trade union oriented body. In the immediate postwar period a number of European countries faced grave threats from extremist groups to the survival of their democratic institutions, including the trade unions, but only Italy succumbed. Later on the deep economic depression of the 1930s brought with it not only widespread unemployment and declining standards of living but also a severe political upheaval which in the end in one way or another destroyed the trade union movements in Germany, Austria, Czechoslovakia, Spain and elsewhere and left many others in gravely weakened condition. In view of the close relationship between political and economic problems, the IFTU and the Labour and Socialist International collaborated intimately on many international issues through formal joint committees as well as through informal channels. As a result the IFTU adopted official positions on almost all important political developments of the time, including the powers and functions of the League of Nations, disarmament, reparations and the war debts, the growth of fascism, Italian aggression against Ethiopia, the war in Spain, collective security and others.

70. As its long term objective the IFTU, like its political counterpart, the Labour and Socialist International, envisaged the establishment of a socialist society through the gradual process of parliamentary democracy. But for the immediate future it stressed the need for a reduction in working hours, more protective labour legislation, measures to combat unemployment, control of national and international cartels, freedom of migration, abolition of restrictions on international trade, and the maintenance of stable currencies. It should also be noted that already in the 1920s and 1930s the IFTU advocated the introduction and expansion of industrial democracy as the counterpart of political democracy. By industrial democracy it understood the establishment of national economic councils with trade union representation and the formation of factory and shop councils along lines developed in the Weimar Republic.

71. Despite initial criticism of the terms of the Peace Treaty establishing the International Labour Organization the IFTU soon became an active supporter of the ILO. Leaders of IFTU national affiliates became the foremost spokesmen for world labour at ILO conferences, and the IFTU contributed many proposals of its own for adoption as international labour conventions. Moreover, the IFTU assumed responsibility for servicing and coordinating the worker group at ILO conferences and Governing Body meetings and achieved effective control over the election of worker representatives to the Governing Body.

72. The general trend in the membership of the IFTU during the 1920s and the first half of the 1930s was downward. Immediately after the end of World War I the affiliated national centres still counted in their ranks a total of about 23,000,000 members. But that figure shrank rapidly from 1920 on until it stabilized at about 13,000,000 by 1924. There it remained for a number of years until the early 1930s when the destruction of the German trade union federation, which alongside the British TUC was the largest IFTU affiliate, brought the total membership down to a low point of about 8,000,000 as of 1934.

73. The decline during the early 1920s had been mainly the result of a shrinking trade union membership among most IFTU affiliates. For example, both the German and British affiliates lost almost half of their 1921 membership by 1925 and 1928, respectively. By contrast with the losses of the 1920s, those of the early 1930s were entirely due to the transformation of the political environment in Germany, Austria, and other countries which led to the destruction of their free trade union movements. The consequences for the IFTU were about the same in either event: a decline in resources and influence. From 1934 on, however, there occurred a resurgence, due partly to the expansion of certain affiliates in the course of economic recovery, partly to the amazing but brief upsurge of members in the French CGT under the Popular Front, and partly to the acquisition of new affiliates, such as the American Federation of Labor in 1937. Total estimated membership thus rose briefly to almost 20,000,000 in the late 1930s, although it is likely that this figure was higher than the number of due paying members.

Membership of International Federation of Trade Unions, 1919–1939

Year	Membership (approximately)
1919	23,000,000
1920	22,700,000
1921	22,000,000
1922	18,000,000
1923	15,300,000
1924	13,000,000
1925	13,400,000
1926	12,800,000
1927	13,000,000
1928	13,500,000
1929	13,700,000
1930	13,000,000
1931	13,700,000
1932	13,700,000
1933	8,500,000
1934	8,200,000
1935	9,000,000
1936	13,000,000
1937	19,500,000
1938	18,000,000
1939	14,000,000

74. It should be pointed out that between 1935 and 1937 the IFTU not only regained most of its earlier membership but also that it succeeded in enlarging the non-European component. Of the 27 affiliates in 1939 nine came from outside Europe. However, efforts by some affiliates to bring the Soviet Union into membership in the 1930s failed when the AUCCTU stipulated a series of unacceptable conditions in the course of negotiations in 1937. The conditions included a demand for a three-headed IFTU presidium in which the AUCCTU would control one of the seats, a second general secretary to be designated by the Russians, and an undertaking that no portion of the dues to be paid by the AUCCTU would be used for propaganda or criticism hostile to the USSR. The IFTU General Council in the first instance and then the Zurich Congress rejected these demands by substantial majorities. Moreover, the AFL had threatened to withdraw from the IFTU if the Russian proposals were granted and the AUCCTU admitted to membership.

75. The AFL had returned to the fold in 1937. Its leaders considered the fascist threat to the democracies and to free trade unionism to be grave enough to override their reluctance for making common cause with the European socialist trade unions. Their decision was also influenced by the rise of a second American trade union federation, the Committee for Industrial Organization (after 1938, the Congress of Industrial Organizations) whose aggressive leaders were aiming at the establishment of their own international ties. By rejoining the IFTU, the AFL prevented the rival CIO from achieving a form of international recognition because of the IFTU's long-standing rule against accepting dual affiliates from one country.

76. A number of significant changes in IFTU administration and leadership occurred in the interwar period which must be noted. German preeminence, which had been so marked before World War I, ceased after the war, and for a few years no Germans were represented among the elected leadership or the secretariat. But no other country was strong enough to claim the succession, and the result was a diffusion of influence among the British TUC, the French CGT, and the secretariat. Originally the secretariat had been directed by two, later three, coequal secretaries, but this arrangement proved to be unsatisfactory. It was abandoned in 1927 when Johann Sassenbach, a German, was designated as General Secretary. His appointment symbolized the return of German influence, although not in the same proportions as during the pre-war period. Sassenbach retired in 1930 and was replaced by Walther Schevenels who retained the position until the dissolution of the IFTU at the end of World War II.

77. A further sign of the return of German influence was the unfortunate decision to move IFTU headquarters from Amsterdam to Berlin. The move took place in 1931 despite the objections of a minority which feared that the political climate in Germany was too unstable. Less than two years later the headquarters had to be shifted once again when it became obvious that the IFTU could not operate unmolested under the Nazi government. In May 1933 the staff hurriedly moved to Paris.

78. During the two interwar decades the governing structure of the IFTU consisted of a Congress which met every two to three years, a General Council (until 1924 called Management Committee) which met annually, and an Executive Committee which met every two months. After the founding congress in Amsterdam in 1919 and an extraordinary congress in London the following year, regular congresses were held in Rome (1922), Vienna (1924), Paris (1927), Stockholm (1930), Brussels (1933), London (1936), and Zurich (1939). Voting rights at congresses were proportionate to the number of paid-up affiliated members. The General Council consisted most of the time of one delegate from each affiliated organization plus the members of the Executive Committee. Its responsibilities extended to an examination of the reports of activities, approval of the programme of action, and decisions on organizational and financial questions. Of generally greater importance for day-to-day affairs was the Executive Committee whose members included the president (invariably furnished by the British TUC), from three to five vice-presidents, and the General Secretary.

79. On the eve of World War II the IFTU held its last congress in Zurich. It passed resolutions against war and against fascist aggression, but events far beyond the reach of the IFTU were determining the course of world events. A few weeks after the Zurich Congress the signing of the Stalin–Hitler Pact destroyed all remaining hopes for peace.

D. International Trade Secretariats (1919–1939)

80. Reconstruction was the first task of the International Trade Secretariats after the war. By 1921 there were again 29 ITSs in operation. Each one specialized in a particular craft or industry, although some of the larger bodies extended across several industries, for example the International Transport Workers' Federation (ITF) and the International Metalworkers' Federation (IMF). A few amalgamations among small and weak ITSs reduced the total number, but the reduction was counterbalanced by the establishment of several new ITSs in the 1930s. Thus by 1939 there were still 27 secretariats.

81. Their overall aims during the interwar period remained unchanged: to improve the conditions of workers in their own sector through international action. That meant channeling financial aid in case of strikes or lockouts, promoting reciprocity arrangements under which union members who moved to another country could readily join their appropriate union and be eligible for its benefits and protection, furthering exchanges of information on wages and working conditions, and extending support to ILO activities concerned with specific industries and occupations. Having been created by socialist trade unions, the ITSs also professed long-range socialist objectives, above all a gradual transition from capitalism to socialism and the nationalization of key industries, but these objectives did not greatly influence their practical work.

82. In organizational and governing arrangements there was a high degree of similarity among the ITSs. Most were managed by a general secretary whose day-to-day administration was supervised by an executive body. General policy was set by a congress which met every two to three years. Almost half of all ITSs had established their headquarters in Germany by 1933. Like the IFTU they were forced to relocate on short notice after the Nazis came to power.

83. There was a close relationship between the membership of the ITSs and the membership of the IFTU. The national centres affiliated with the IFTU were expected as a matter of policy to urge their affiliated unions to join the appropriate ITS. In turn, unions affiliated with an ITS but belonging to a national centre not yet affiliated with the IFTU were asked to use their influence to help bring about such an affiliation.

84. In contrast to the policy of the IFTU, which ordinarily admitted not more than one national trade union centre, the ITSs were generally willing to accept membership from more than one union in a particular country. This policy was made necessary by the fact that the jurisdictional lines at international level did not necessarily correspond with the lines at national level. For instance, the International Transport Workers' Federation was concerned with all forms of transportation – rail, sea, air, and road – but in many countries these sectors were organized by separate unions. In some instances a reverse situation arose when a national union with an industrially or occupationally diversified membership took out affiliations in more than one ITS.

85. For several years in the 1920s the prospective membership of Russian unions became an issue of some controversy. Most ITSs took positions against such affiliation on the basis that the AUCCTU first had to join the IFTU before the ITSs would consider an affiliation from an individual Russian union. Two secretariats – the ITF and IMF – entered into negotiations which eventually failed. A third, the International Union of Workers in the Food and Drink Trades, did accept a Russian union into membership in 1922, but the relationship was a difficult one until the Russians withdrew in 1929.

86. Despite close affinities, the ties between the ITSs and the IFTU were not entirely without friction. Under an agreement concluded in 1922 the ITSs were not to concern themselves with the formulation of general policies since this area belonged to the IFTU but were expected to adhere to IFTU views and insofar as possible to implement them. The agreement also gave the ITSs representation at IFTU congresses but not voting rights. (In a temporary departure from the rule on voting rights, the Vienna IFTU Congress of 1924 decided to admit three ITS representatives with voting rights to the General Council. This arrangement, however, lasted only until the Paris Congress in 1927 when it was eliminated on the ground that three ITS representatives could not adequately represent all the ITSs.)

87. The basic problem in the relationship was the existence, side by side, of two different principles of organization which, in turn, led to different policy emphases despite a common ideological basis. Indeed, some spokesmen for ITS interests envisaged a structure of international trade union organization built entirely on ITS components instead of national centres. Others, taking a somewhat less extreme view, wanted to continue the two organizational principles by reconstructing the IFTU so as to include both the national centres and the ITS as its basic units. These and other proposals remained topics of discussion at most IFTU congresses, but in the end the only tangible result was a decision that there should be an annual conference of ITSs to be held in conjunction with the meeting of the IFTU General Council. The ITSs thus continued to pursue their industrial activities independently of, but as far as possible in close touch with, the IFTU. They maintained their autonomy, but on issues that transcended the competence of any particular ITS they recognized the right of the IFTU to articulate the collective views of the movement as a whole.

E. International Federation of Christian Trade Unions (1920–1939)

88. Christian labour organizations were established in several European countries before the turn of the century, particularly among textile workers, white collars employees and coal miners. National federations composed of Christian unions emerged before World War I (in some countries shortly after its end) in Germany, the Netherlands, France, Belgium, Austria, Italy and Switzerland.

89. In most countries Christian trade unionism was closely identified with the teachings of the Catholic church, although in a few, notably the Netherlands, Germany, and Switzerland, it contained important Protestant components. In philosophy it was as opposed to capitalism and its liberalist heritage as it condemned socialism, communism, and anarcho-syndicalism. It emphasized spiritual as against material values, brotherhood and class cooperation as against the class struggle, and in particular it stressed the ennoblement of the individual personality as the goal of all economic and social organizations. Private property, nation, church, and class were to be regarded as legitimate institutions whose existence was intended to serve the spiritual perfectibility of every human being. Upon these principles Christian trade unionism espoused harmonious relations with employers, protective labour legislation, responsible collective bargaining, a living wage, and eventually a system of bipartite councils to determine the conditions of production, distribution, and employment in each industry.

90. National differences existed chiefly between German emphasis on centralist structures and interconfessional membership versus French preferences for decentralization and close adherence to Catholic doctrine. The war caused the same personal and organizational cleavages between national Christian trade union movements as occurred between the socialist organizations, and it was only with difficulty that an organizing committee could bring the several national organizations together in The Hague in 1920 to establish the International Federation of Christian Trade Unions (abbreviated here by its French initials CISC to avoid confusion).

91. The founding congress was attended by the following organizations:

Countries	Membership
Belgium	150,000
Germany	1,250,000
France	140,000
Hungary	189,000
Italy	1,250,000
Netherlands (Protestant Unions)	73,400
Netherlands (Catholic Unions)	170,000
Austria	59,000
Spain	60,000
Czechoslovakia	7,500
Switzerland	17,500
	3,366,400

After The Hague, CISC congresses took place in Innsbruck (1922), Lucerne (1925), Munich (1928), Antwerp (1932), Montreux (1934), and Paris (1937). As in the case of the IFTU, the neutral countries had to furnish the leadership in the first few postwar years. Dutch trade unionists took the secretary and treasurer positions, and a Swiss was elected as the first president. The governing structure established in The Hague resembled that of the IFTU. It consisted of a triennial Congress, an International Council with one delegate for each affiliate, and an Executive Committee of five members which included the General Secretary.

92. In the course of the 1920s the CISC lost about half its membership because of the overall decline in unionization during the decade and also because of the destruction of its Italian affiliate. Additional serious losses occurred during the 1930s with the demise of the German and Austrian contingents. By the end of the interwar period, the remaining centres of genuine strength were limited to Belgium, France, and the Netherlands. Smaller affiliates also existed in Switzerland, Luxemburg, Czechoslovakia, Hungary and Yugoslavia. Organization outside of Europe had barely begun.

93. Alongside its national affiliates the CISC established a group of trade secretariats similar in purpose to the International Trade Secretariats but organizationally far more integrated into the CISC by according them a constitutionally protected place in the structure of policy-making bodies. In due course 15 such organizations were set up, though none was ever able to achieve great importance within its industry.

94. Relations between the CISC and IFTU were most of the time unfriendly, if not hostile. The ideological gap was too wide. Besides, the tolerance of the dominant trade unions for dual organization, i.e. for pluralism, has always been extremely limited – nationally and internationally. For a brief time in the 1930s the common danger posed by totalitarianism forced the two groups closer together, and as a gesture of goodwill the IFTU sponsored the CISC General Secretary, P. J. S. Serrarens, for a seat as a deputy worker member on the ILO Governing Body. The detente, however, lasted only a short time. What one group regarded as its right to an independent existence was seen by the other as an almost treasonable act against working class unity.

Chapter III. The Historical Background since 1939

I. Reorganization, Unity and Rift (1939–1949)

A. Wartime Realignments

95. Within a year of the outbreak of World War II, IFTU headquarters had to be moved from Paris to the relative safety of London. There a group of leading IFTU and ITS officials established, in 1942, an Emergency International Trade Union Council (EITUC) as a temporary replacement for the inactive IFTU governing bodies. The EITUC was to consider pressing international issues and to voice the collective views of international labour.

96. As host to the IFTU, as its largest affiliate, and as an organization with broad international experience, the British TUC under the leadership of its General Secretary, Walter Citrine, assumed a leading role in international trade unionism during the war. Its preeminent role was further reinforced by the creation, at TUC initiative, of several binational trade union committees outside the framework of the IFTU. The first one was the Anglo-French Trade Union Council of 1939–40 which, however, did not survive the collapse of France. The second and considerably more important one established a link with the Soviet labour organizations after the USSR had been drawn into the military conflict. That body, the Anglo-Soviet Trade Union Council, held its first meeting in October 1941 in the Soviet Union. The third one, the Anglo-American Trade Union Committee, was established in 1942. On the American side it covered only the AFL which had insisted on excluding the rival CIO from such a body. The first meeting of this committee took place in Washington in February 1943.

97. The most important question for these groups, next to labour's contribution to the war effort, was the prospective structure of the postwar international labour movement. That question, in turn, had a procedural and a substantive aspect. On the procedural side, the proper institutional channels for making the basic substantive decisions had to be determined. The IFTU had a legitimate claim that was strongly supported by several affiliates, foremost among them the AFL. Consonant with this claim the EITUC set up a committee to draft a programme for the reconstruction of the international labour movement. However, a contrary view was forwarded by the AUCCTU and CIO. Deeming the IFTU in which they held no membership to be in some sense a discredited organization, both sought to shift the decision-making process into a forum that would be less subject to being influenced by the traditions and principles of the prewar international trade union movement. They proposed that a world trade union conference be convened by the British TUC rather than the IFTU.

98. Ultimately it was the TUC's responsiveness to the pressures from the AUCCTU and the CIO that decided the outcome. Such factors as expectations of enduring postwar labour unity and the hope of helping to promote a stable peace through concerted labour action played an important role in the decision. Also, the TUC may have assumed that it could in the end persuade the AFL to abandon its opposition to collaboration with the AUCCTU and the CIO. In any event, the 1943 Trades Union Congress endorsed a resolution authorizing the General Council to convene a world trade union conference under TUC auspices and thus bypassing the IFTU.

99. On the substantive side the major issues to be resolved included:
1. The perpetuation or revitalization of the IFTU, with or without internal changes, versus the creation of an entirely new body;
2. the prospective admission or exclusion of national centres from Communist countries, especially the AUCCTU;
3. the maintenance of the rule admitting only one national centre per country versus a more flexible policy;
4. the proposed structural integration of the ITSs into the international federation versus their continued autonomy; and
5. the future role of Christian unions.

B. Formation of the World Federation of Trade Unions (1945)

100. These and other issues were in the forefront of discussions at the TUC-convened world trade union conference that met in London in February 1945, although only the first two points were definitely resolved. The conference was attended by 135 delegates and 30 observers representing 40 national trade union centres from the Allied Powers, 17 delegates from international bodies (including the IFTU), and 9 observers from neutral countries. Present also was the Latin American Confederation of Workers (CTAL) that had been founded in 1938 by Vicente Lombardo Toledano and that under his leadership became a Communist-oriented organization. The total claimed membership represented by the London gathering was about 50,000,000; over half of this figure was accounted for by the AUCCTU alone.

101. In the absence of the AFL, which had persisted in its position, the principal trade union centres on the scene were the TUC, the CIO, and the AUCCTU. The letter of invitation issued by the TUC had stressed that the conference was to be 'purely exploratory and consultative'. In fact, however, under the aggressive leadership of the CIO and AUCCTU the TUC's entreaties to make no irreversible decisions were disregarded, and the conference committed itself to a line of action that would inevitably lead to the creation of a new world labour body in place of the IFTU. This decision was sealed by the appointment of a 41-member committee charged with

1. acting as an interim authority for international labour,
2. representing its interests before national governments and international agencies,
3. drafting a constitution for the new organization, and
4. convening another world conference before the end of 1945.

102. Because of its large size, the committee chosen in London elected a smaller administrative committee to perform the required work. Its major task was the preparation of a constitution for a new world labour body, an assignment which it completed well ahead of schedule. The new organization, to be known as the World Federation of Trade Unions (WFTU), was to be open to all bona fide national trade union centres, but the draft did not specify what was to be understood by bona fide. Normally there was to be only one national affiliate per country, but exceptions could be made where justifiable. As had already been the case in the IFTU, the autonomy of WFTU affiliates was guaranteed, and the execution of WFTU decisions was left to their compliance. The International Trade Secretariats, however, were to become integrated components of the WFTU, subject to its authority and rules.

103. The WFTU governing structure was to consist of a biennial world congress where the voting rights of delegates would be roughly proportionate to membership represented; a somewhat smaller General Council that would meet annually and act in lieu of the congress; an Executive Committee of 22 members; an Executive Bureau composed of the WFTU chairman, seven vice-chairmen, and the general secretary; and finally a secretariat with a general secretary and three assistant general secretaries. It was evident from the outset that in this elaborate structure the effective power centre would be located in the Executive Bureau and the secretariat.

104. A second world trade union conference met in Paris in September–October 1945 to adopt the constitution of the new World Federation of Trade Unions, designate the officers and staff, and make other necessary decisions to begin operation. In attendance were 187 delegates from 65 organizations in 56 countries as well as observers from the ITSs, the IFTU, the International Federation of Christian Trade Unions (CISC), and other bodies. The total number of members represented was claimed to be 67,000,000. Controversial issues still to be resolved included the location of WFTU headquarters and the position of the ITSs in the new structure. Paris was chosen as WFTU headquarters despite the objections of several delegations that were fearful of undue influence on the WFTU by the Communist-dominated French CGT. The relationship of the ITSs to the WFTU was left to be decided in subsequent negotiations. For the post of WFTU general secretary Louis Saillant of the French CGT was selected. Walther Schevenels, the head of the IFTU before and during the war, became one of three assistant general secretaries, the other two being an American and a Russian. Walter Citrine of the TUC was elected as the first chairman.

105. The affairs of the IFTU were wound up at a final meeting of its General Council in December 1945 in London. The AFL, absent from the meeting, had already made known its opposition to the dissolution on the ground that only a congress was constitutionally entitled to take such action. But all the other delegates in attendance represented organizations that had already become affiliated with the WFTU. They were unwilling to be distracted by fine points of constitutional procedure. The IFTU ceased to exist as of 31 December 1945.

106. During the next three years the AFL went its separate way, though not toward isolation. On the contrary, it became extraordinarily active in international labour affairs. It stationed representatives in European and Asian countries to assist trade unions to reestablish their forces. It also contributed to the rebuilding of the ITSs. And in the Western hemisphere it created an independent regional labour organization (the Inter-American Confederation of Labor, or CIT) as a counterforce to Lombardo Toledano's CTAL.

C. Discord in the WFTU (1945–1949)

107. The membership of the WFTU at the time of its founding was represented to be about 65,000,000. The only substantial changes which occurred in the 1945–49 period resulted from increases in the membership of affiliated organizations, particularly those in Eastern Europe, rather than from new acquisitions. Some applications for admission were deferred after the WFTU became involved in severe internal controversies. Nevertheless it is evident that the WFTU started off on a much larger scale numerically and geographically than was ever attained by the IFTU. (The major absences were the AFL, the Christian trade union centres, and later the newly formed trade union organizations in the two postwar Germanys.) But the scale also reflected a substantial amount of diversity among affiliates in terms of traditions, political loyalties, and conceptions of trade unionism. In particular, large differences soon emerged between a bloc of Western trade unions under the leadership of the TUC and CIO and another bloc of Communist-led organizations located mainly in Eastern Europe but also including unions in France, Italy, Latin America, and Asia. Numerically, the second bloc was by far the larger one, and from the very beginning its representation in the governing organs of the WFTU was correspondingly greater. But during the first phase of the WFTU's existence, that is from 1945 to 1947, the differences were still largely submerged by a common effort to demonstrate the feasibility of world labour unity and by restraint on the Communist side in the exercise of its numerical superiority.

108. The aims of the WFTU, as formally stated in its constitution, included commitments

a. to unite the trade unions of the whole world, irrespective of race, nationality, religion or political opinion;
b. to assist workers in less developed countries to establish their organizations;
c. to combat fascism and war;
d. to represent labour interests in international institutions; and
e. to promote democratic liberties, full employment, improved wages and working conditions, and social security.

These were ambitious goals, but were not intended to be taken literally. In practice the prospects of the WFTU depended on a sustained degree of internal agreement. That was achieved only in the beginning. By 1947 it had become evident that the political differences which increasingly separated governments West and East were producing parallel differences at the level of national trade union organizations.

109. The touchstone of conflict in the WFTU was the European Recovery Programme, better known as the Marshall Plan. Almost uniformly the trade unions in Western countries hailed it from its inception in 1947 as a way of overcoming serious obstacles to the reconstruction of the war-devastated European economies, while the labour organizations in Eastern Europe followed the Soviet lead of opposing the programme as a scheme of American capitalism to dominate Europe. It was during this period that the Communist majority in the WFTU's executive and administrative bodies began to demonstrate its superior position. The WFTU secretariat under General Secretary Louis Saillant controlled the contents of the WFTU publications, including the *Information Bulletin*, and the Communist side had a five-to-four majority in the Executive Bureau as well as a twelve-to-nine majority in the Executive Committee. Consequently WFTU publications contained numerous attacks on the Marshall Plan and on its trade union supporters, and the demands of Western trade unions for a discussion of the Marshall Plan in WFTU executive organs were consistently rejected.

110. Unable to obtain satisfaction inside the WFTU, the Western trade unions then organized their own conference in London in March 1948 to discuss the means by which trade unions could contribute to the success of the Marshall Plan. For the first time in any international trade union meeting both Americal national centres, the AFL and CIO, were represented, thus signalling the impending end of their long-standing differences on domestic and international affairs and underscoring the importance of the meeting. The conference established a permanent administrative body in the form of a Trade Union Advisory Committee to the European Recovery Programme.

111. While the differences over the Marshall Plan were separating the two blocs in the WFTU, the negotiations for incorporating the International Trade Secretariats into a single WFTU-controlled structure were nearing failure. At the formation of the WFTU in 1945 approximately 25 ITSs that had survived the war were just beginning to reconstruct their organizations. Article 13 of the WFTU constitution provided for their eventual integration into the WFTU as subordinate bodies under the new collective title of International Trade Departments, but the specific terms on which the autonomous ITSs were to dissolve themselves and accept the authority of the WFTU still had to be separately negotiated. The initial WFTU-prepared draft of these terms was unsatisfactory to the ITSs, and protracted as well as difficult negotiations then ensued. These ended in September 1948 with a final refusal by the ITSs to accept an end to their autonomous status. In their tenacious negotiating position the ITSs received strong encouragement from the AFL and from unions affiliated with the AFL that from 1945 on had begun to join their appropriate Trade Secretariats. The ITSs were also deterred from accepting integration by the evidence of rising discord in the WFTU and Communist control over WFTU policies.

112. The internal differences in the WFTU became steadily more acute in the fall of 1948 and increasingly pointed toward ultimate separation. It ought to be recalled that they were influenced not only by the escalating controversy over the Marshall Plan, the Berlin blockade, and other signs of serious East–West tensions, but also by splits in the French and Italian national trade union centres between Communist and anti-Communist groups, a similar split in the Berlin trade unions, and a sharp turn toward a more decisive anti-Communist position by the leadership of the American CIO and the British TUC.

113. An irrevocable breakup occurred at the January 1949 meeting of the Executive Bureau in Paris. On this occasion the TUC, seconded by the CIO, proposed a one-year suspension of WFTU activities as a cooling-off period. The possibility of a renewed start-up was to be contingent on intervening developments in East–West relations. The proposal was rejected by the representatives of Communist trade unions and General Secretary Saillant, whereupon the Executive Bureau members from the Western countries left the meeting. During the next several months all Western WFTU affiliates except those under Communist leadership and many organizations from the developed countries announced their withdrawal from the organization. Numerically, the unions that remained constituted a majority of individual members, though not of organizations. To compensate for the losses they now admitted a number of national centres whose applications for affiliation had been deferred. Later that year, that is in June 1949, the WFTU held its second world congress in Milan.

D. Emergence of the International Confederation of Free Trade Unions (1949)

114. The split in the WFTU created a vacuum that was soon to be filled by the formation of a new trade union international. However, its establishment was contingent on the solution of several issues, notably those involving the relations between AFL and CIO, the role of Christian trade unions in a new federation, and the relationship of the ITSs to the new federation. It took most of the remainder of 1949, including a preparatory conference in Geneva in June 1949, to resolve them. The terms of the relationship between AFL and CIO were clarified by the decision of the AFL to recognize the CIO as an equal partner in international labour affairs. The Christian trade unions were offered an opportunity (which ultimately they refused) to join the new organization on condition that they would in due course cease their affiliation with a separate Christian international. The autonomous existence of the ITSs was recognized under mutually satisfactory conditions that envisaged close and continuing consultations and ITS representation in ICFTU deliberative and executive bodies.

115. The preparatory Geneva conference in June 1949 had appointed a committee to work out the formation of a new world labour organization. On call of this committee a conference of national trade union centres met in London from 28 November to 9 December 1949. It was attended by 261 delegates from 59 national federations representing a total claimed membership of 48,000,000. (The actual number of affiliates at the start was 67, but not all were represented at the founding congress.) Among the countries represented for the first time in the postwar period was a strong West German contingent. On 7 December, the delegates adopted the constitution of the International Confederation of Free Trade Unions (ICFTU). The preamble of the constitution emphasized a commitment to social justice, full employment, freedom of association, political democracy, and aid to trade unions in the less developed countries. All bona fide national centres were declared eligible for membership, and their autonomy was guaranteed. Other important provisions of the constitution will be referred to in a separate chapter on the ICFTU (see below), but mention must be made here of the unprecedented decision to establish within the overall ICFTU framework separate regional organizations for the major areas of the world.

116. The London conference was strongly influenced by the presence of the two American national centres whose expectations about the proper role of an international trade union federation now coincided very closely. These expectations emphasized a philosophy of trade unionism free of dependence on parties, governments, employers, churches or other institutions, a vigorous defence of free trade unionism wherever it came under attack, a militant anti-Communist position, a concentration of resources on the establishment of trade unions in less developed areas, and a balanced distribution of influence and power within the ICFTU so that no single area would exercise a preponderant role. Although European trade unions agreed in principle with these expectations, differences in interpretation and practical implementation were later on to cause difficulties.

117. It was with strong support from AFL and CIO that the first ICFTU congress chose as its general secretary J. H. Oldenbroek, the leader of the International Transport Workers Federation, who had led the ITSs in their successful resistance against integration into the WFTU. Brussels was chosen as headquarters, at least in part for the purpose of avoiding any suspicion of domination of the secretariat by one of the larger affiliates. Paul Finet, a Belgian, was elected as the first president. He had chaired the Geneva Preparatory Conference and the founding congress and was generally recognized as an exceedingly able trade union leader.

E. Reconstitution of the Christian Trade Union International (1945–1949)

118. Even more so than in the case of the IFTU the Christian trade union international (CISC) was compelled to cease its activities during World War II after its headquarters in Utrecht, the Netherlands, came under German occupation. When the TUC issued its invitations to the February 1945 London conference, it included CISC affiliates in France, Belgium, the Netherlands (already partly liberated by that time), and Switzerland, but not the CISC itself. It was anticipated at the time that the CISC could be induced to dissolve itself, but that turned out to be a miscalculation. Later in the year the future of a separate Christian international came up again at the founding congress of the WFTU in Paris. This time the CISC had been invited and was officially present up to the moment of the founding of the WFTU, but in the end neither the CISC nor its affiliates were prepared to submerge their separate existence for the sake of labour unity. Actually by that time the CISC's decision to rebuild its organization had already been taken at a congress, the eighth one, that had met in October 1945 in Brussels. Having made its decision, the CISC offered its cooperation to the WFTU, but only on condition of equality between the two. This offer, however, had little practical significance since during the 1945–1949 period the WFTU was not interested in such collaboration.

119. Although the reconstruction of the CISC as an international body was achieved by 1949, the base of the organization became substantially smaller as compared to the 1920s and 1930s. Efforts to promote the reemergence of Christian unions in Germany, Austria, and Italy, which had at one time constituted important parts of the overall organization, failed to overcome the stronger appeal of labour unity, strongly endorsed by the occupation authorities, although eventually a small Christian labour group did form in Germany. More successful were the rebuilding efforts of the surviving Christian trade unions in France (CFTC, later CFDT), Belgium (CSC), and the Netherlands (NKV and CNV). By the time of the tenth CISC congress in Lyons in 1949 it was evident that these three countries with their four labour movements would henceforth constitute the indispensable basis for the continued existence of the CISC.

II. Major Developments Since 1950

120. From 1949 on the history of international trade union organizations became to a substantial extent, although not entirely, the history of rival efforts between ICFTU and WFTU to gain adherents, influence, and prestige. The CISC stood largely apart from this contest because its small size, limited resources, and lack of clear identification with a major power bloc minimized its ability – and perhaps also its drive – to play a visibly significant role.

A. The International Confederation of Free Trade Unions

121. The principal concerns of the ICFTU in the initial decade of its existence were the development of a workable administrative and policy-setting machinery, the creation of regional organizations, the quest for new affiliates in the less developed parts of the world, the maintenance of harmonious relations with its main constituents in Europe and America, the demarcation of responsibilities between itself and the ITSs, and the formulation of generally acceptable policies on major issues, such as decolonization, economic aid, human rights, communism, East–West relations, defence and disarmament, and others. All of these endeavours were complicated by the basic nature of the ICFTU as a loose confederation of autonomous affiliates held together, by no means always tightly, by a shared belief in the principles of free trade unionism and by a common rejection of totalitarian ideology.

122. The highest policy making body, the Congress had originally been mandated to meet biennially, but for economy reasons that requirement was later changed to three-year, and even more recently to four-year intervals. Because congresses tend to become milestones in the history of an organization, those that were held after the founding Congress in London in 1949 should be noted here: Milan (1951), Stockholm (1953), Vienna (1955), Tunis (1957), Brussels (1959), Berlin (1962), Amsterdam (1965), Brussels (1969), London (1972), Mexico City (1975), and Madrid (1979). The General Council, first intended as a smaller version of the congress but with some functions of its own, met only once – in Berlin in 1952. It was abolished at the Stockholm Congress in conjunction with an increase in the membership of the Executive Board.

123. In effect, it was the Executive Board and its subcommittees that became the real policy-making instruments of the ICFTU. That development required a balance among the different constituent areas on the Board, and it took several adjustments to achieve a composition that reflected both the worldwide scope of the organization and the claims of its largest and most influential affiliates for a special role. To satisfy a host of regional and national demands for seats on the Executive Board, the number of members was gradually increased from 19 to 29, with equivalent increases in the number of first and second substitutes.

124. As the highest full-time officer, the general secretary from the very start occupied a key position, and perforce he had to be a man of many talents including administrative competence, linguistic skills, negotiating ability, and unusual endurance. For the first eleven years the office was held by J. H. Oldenbroek, a Dutch national and previously the general secretary of the International Transport Workers Federation. He had distinguished himself by leading the struggle of the ITSs to remain independent of the WFTU and had acquired a wealth of experience in international trade union organization. His departure in 1960 was the consequence of growing discontent on the part of his former supporters in the United States who felt that the ICFTU lacked vitality and who insisted that a change in leadership was necessary to strengthen the organization. The American view was not shared by most European affiliates, although eventually enough of them became doubtful to make Oldenbroek's position untenable. In retrospect there is little question that despite his shortcomings he was an exceedingly able person. Oldenbroek's successor was Omer Becu who also came out of the ITF where he had served at one time under Oldenbroek. Becu, a Belgian, at first had strong American endorsement but he, too, was ultimately unable to measure up to American expectations some of which were highly unrealistic. He left office in 1967. His successor was Harm Buiter, a national of the Netherlands, whose previous international trade union experience had been chiefly at European regional level. Buiter's tenure lasted for only a few years. He became embroiled in a bitter dispute with the AFL–CIO over the handling of the application of the United Automobile Workers Union for direct membership in the ICFTU, and it was during his administration that the AFL–CIO severed its ties. He resigned in 1971 and was followed early in 1972 by Otto Kersten, the present holder of the position, who until then had been in charge of international affairs in the central office of the German DGB.

125. An initial problem of major importance for the ICFTU was the creation of regional organizations and their proper relationship to the central office. The initiative for regional subgroupings, an innovation in the structure of international trade unionism, came originally from the labour organizations in the United States and the underdeveloped areas. It was their objective, in part, to neutralize the historic predominance of European labour in the international labour movement and to develop a means of coping with specific regional problems more effectively than a highly centralized body could. However, acceptance of the principle of regionalization still left open the question of the relationship between the central Secretariat and the regional bodies, and notably the degree of autonomy to be accorded to the regional bodies. This matter will be further discussed in a subsequent chapter.

126. The first regional body, established in 1950, was the European Regional Organization (ERO). It was followed by the Western Hemisphere where the Interamerican Regional Organization of Workers (ORIT) was set up in 1951. (North American labour, including Canada, played a leading role in the establishment of ORIT. In fact, ORIT absorbed a previously existing organization for the American hemisphere, the CIT, which the AFL had established in 1948 as an adversary to the Communist-inspired CTAL.) The Asian Regional Organization (ARO) was founded later in the same year, 1951, but it took until 1960 for an African Regional Organization (AFRO) to be established.

127. Of these four regional bodies two no longer exist. ERO was almost from the very beginning faced with two difficult sets of problems. One was the ability of most of its member organizations to take care of their own affairs without requiring external assistance from a regional body. When a vast field of activity did open up in the 1950s in conjunction with the formation of the European supranational bodies – especially the European Coal and Steel Authority, the Common Market, and the European Free Trade Association – ERO affiliates became involved in internal differences along the same lines that divided their governments into the Group of Six (the European Economic Community) and the Group of Seven (the European Free Trade Association). This division prevented ERO from becoming European labour's single and exclusive regional spokesman. After an interval of trying to get along with fragmented structures, there finally did emerge a determination to forge a unified European organization, but this objective could be attained only at the expense of ERO. The act of formally dissolving ERO occurred in 1969. Its place nowadays is occupied by the independent European Trade Union Confederation which will be discussed below.

128. In Africa the creation of a regional organization encountered almost from the very start serious difficulties caused by governments and the proponents of an exclusive pan-African ideology. During the period of rapid decolonization in the 1950s and early 1960s the ICFTU had taken a vigorous stand in favour of rapid extension of national independence. This stand earned the ICFTU widespread support from African unions, and for a time AFRO became a rallying point for African unions seeking to retain an autonomous position in their own countries during the post-independence period. Free trade unionism, however, did not appear to be an important or even a desirable goal to most African governments. On the contrary, they tended to regard the international ties of their labour organizations as an impediment to their ability to obtain compliance with government policies. To create an alternative to AFRO, a number of African states under Ghanaian leadership encouraged their labour movements to establish in 1961 a separate pan-African labour organization, the All-African Trade Union Federation (AATUF). Although AATUF encountered serious difficulties, especially after the overthrow of Kwame Nkrumah in Ghana in 1966, its objective of eliminating the ICFTU's influence in Africa came to be shared by an increasing number of African governments. The ICFTU gradually lost a substantial portion of its African affiliates, and in 1965 the affairs of AFRO came under the direct supervision of the ICFTU general secretary, a step equivalent to being placed in trusteeship.

Following a period of suspended existence, the African Regional Organization was reactivated in 1972 at the urging of the ICFTU's few remaining African affiliates. However, recent developments hostile to free trade unionism in such countries as Ethiopia and Nigeria, where the ICFTU used to have some of its staunchest affiliates, make it appear unlikely that in the foreseeable future AFRO can become a viable organization. That conclusion is underscored by the formation in 1972 of the Organization of African Trade Union Unity (OATUU) as the official trade union branch of the intergovernmental Organization of African Unity.

129. By contrast with ERO and AFRO, the ICFTU's regional organizations for the Americas and Asia – ORIT and ARO – have had an uninterrupted existence to the present time. In the case of ORIT this was due in part to the financial and organizational support from its affiliates in the United States and Canada, although subsidies from Brussels headquarters have also been needed for organizational, educational, and other activities. Among Latin American affiliates those from Mexico and Venezuela have been organizationally and financially the most stable. From its very inception ORIT has had to contend with rival organizations. Under the first Perón government Argentina sponsored a regional body, ATLAS, whose purpose it was to disseminate Peronist influence throughout the hemisphere. ATLAS did not survive the fall of Perón, but there have always been other rival organizations sponsored by Communist and radical ex-Christian groups. Nevertheless, since its formation ORIT has claimed to be the most representative regional labour body. Currently it reports 32 member organizations. ORIT's most serious problem has been the continent-wide struggle for the existence of independent trade unionism. Many Latin American regimes have suppressed or otherwise impeded their labour organizations, and although occasionally an authoritarian regime has been superseded by a more or less democratic one, the general trend has been toward more rather than fewer restraints.

130. The Asian Regional Organization (ARO) was established in 1951. This part of the world, compared with others, encompasses the widest range of diversity in terms of the social, political, and economic development of the various countries in the region. Consequently, it has not been easy for ARO to instill in its members a strong sense of identification with the destiny of the region. The tendency among unions, that constantly reasserts itself, is to concentrate their attention on the national level. Moreover, for many years the resources of the ICFTU's Asian affiliates were insufficient to make their regional organization self-supportive. That meant dependence on subsidies from ICFTU headquarters. In recent years, however, that situation with all its attendant difficulties, has gradually changed in proportion to the steadily increasing strength and self-reliance of ICFTU affiliates in Japan, Malaysia, Singapore, Turkey, and several other countries. ARO has become stronger and has benefitted from a substantial increase in membership. When ARO first began to operate it had affiliates in nine countries. By 1961, it included 27 organizations from 15 countries, representing some six million members.

Although growth since then has been less spectacular – it now has affiliates in 19 countries, including Israel – the internal stability of most affiliated organizations has increased, as has the effectiveness of the regional organization.

131. Supplementing the work of its regional bodies the ICFTU concentrated a major portion of its own resources in money and staff during the decade of the 1950s on so-called regional activities, a term generally understood to mean educational and organizational work in the less developed areas. The chief assumptions underlying this work were that trade unions were bound to arise and increase in these areas, that external aid could accelerate the process and channel it into the proper directions, and that failure to act would merely be an invitation to other forces to seek a foothold in the trade unions. Partly as a result of regional activities a distinct increase in ICFTU membership occurred in the 1950s, much of it in Third World countries. From an organization which in 1949 grouped only 67 affiliates in 51 countries with a total membership of 48 million, the ICFTU had by 1962 grown to 137 organizations in 106 countries with a total membership of 56 million. However, 1962 constituted the peak year, and thereafter a steady decline set in, especially in the African area for reasons already noted.

132. Particularly strong support for regional activities came from the ICFTU's affiliates in the United States which regarded such work as an indispensable part of decolonization and also as necessary for holding on to ICFTU affiliates and attracting new ones in the Third World. Although some European organizations, notably those in countries with substantial colonial holdings, were at first reluctant to endorse a major ICFTU effort of regional activities, the major policy differences that developed between Americans and Europeans involved organizing strategy. By and large, American unionists emphasized the importance of strengthening the national federations because of their political importance in the pre- and post-independence periods. British unionists were more inclined to stress grass-roots organizing for local-level negotiations with employers. These policy differences led American labour increasingly to regard ICFTU regional efforts as insufficient and prompted the establishment of so-called bilateral activities. This term denoted efforts on the part of the AFL–CIO (and later on of other national centres as well) to engage in their own regional activities, usually through specially created institutions under their control. Inevitably such efforts on the part of individual national centres came into competition with the work of the ICFTU itself. Indeed, from the ICFTU's point of view the resources which the AFL–CIO, the German DGB, and other ICFTU affiliates devoted to their own overseas activities should more properly have been channelled through the ICFTU. However there was very little that the ICFTU could do to control and limit bilateral activities other than to accept them as a *fait accompli* and as far as possible to secure for itself a coordinating function.

133. Relations with the ITSs constituted from the very beginning of the ICFTU in 1949 an area of great importance and also of considerable difficulty.

The existence of basic identity of interests between the two was recognized in the ICFTU constitution. That document further specified that arrangements should be made for the most effective cooperation between them. To carry out that mandate an agreement for mutual cooperation was concluded (the Milan Agreement of 1951) in which the ICFTU affirmed the autonomy of the ITSs, while they in turn acknowledged the authority of the ICFTU in setting policy for both sides on major issues. The agreement was reinforced by provisions for reciprocal representation on executive and plenary bodies. Nevertheless on several occasions sharp differences arose in the 1950s and the first half of the 1960s over the proper pattern of relationships, the allocation of resources for regional activities, the limits of ITS autonomy, and the demarcation of the respective functions. More recently, however, these differences have narrowed, and a revision of the Milan Agreement satisfying ITS demands was ratified by the Ninth ICFTU Congress in 1969. Its essential provisions will be spelled out in another chapter.

134. The maintenance of effective relations with ICFTU affiliates was a complex task for an organization whose two principal constituent blocs – Europeans and Americans – held rather differing views on a substantial number of major issues. Already within two years of the founding congress there was a major clash with the AFL which led that organization to boycott ICFTU meetings for just about all of 1952. Although that particular estrangement was overcome, frictions between the ICFTU and the AFL–CIO recurred frequently and culminated in 1969 in the decision of the AFL–CIO to terminate its affiliation. Ultimately, the overriding issues in controversy were the appropriate degree of anti-Communist militancy to be shown by the ICFTU and its affiliates, the direction of organizing activities in less developed countries to which reference has already been made, and the balance of power in the ICFTU.

135. On the question of how best to deal with communism and other forces hostile to free and democratic unions the American side consistently advocated a policy of complete non-recognition. Although in this matter the declarations of ICFTU congresses and executive bodies were invariably in accord with American views, it was impossible for the ICFTU to make its autonomous affiliates conform to ICFTU resolutions. Because increasing numbers of ICFTU member organizations established contacts with labour organizations in Communist countries in the 1960s, the contradiction between ICFTU policies on the one hand and the practices of several important European affiliates on the other became ever wider and from the viewpoint of the AFL–CIO ever more unacceptable.

136. Regarding the balance of power in the ICFTU, an understanding had been reached when the ICFTU was formed that no regional bloc and no large organization would ever seek to occupy a hegemonic position. The AFL, which was highly sensitive on this point, deemed that understanding to have been broken as early as 1951 when the British TUC successfully promoted the candidacy of its general secretary, Vincent Tewson, for the largely honorary office of ICFTU president. This controversy ended when Tewson decided not to seek reelection on expiration of his two-year term. Nevertheless, other occasions arose in the 1950s and 1960s that to the Americans appeared to tilt the balance of power to their disadvantage. At times they were able to neutralize the incontestable numerical superiority of the European bloc by forming an external alliance with trade unions from the less developed areas, but over the long pull the European side could usually prevail, provided only that it remained united. Moreover, the predominance of the Europeans in the ICFTU administration seemed to more than make up for their occasional defeats on policy issues in plenary sessions. In the end a sense of being permanently in the minority contributed heavily to the disaffection of the AFL–CIO and played a major underlying role in its decision to leave the ICFTU. The Europeans, for their part, resented the domineering attitudes of the top AFL–CIO spokesmen, and felt that the Americans had been given ample satisfaction on their complaints. It was, in short, an unhappy marriage.

B. World Federation of Trade Unions

137. The exit of the free trade unions in 1949 transformed the WFTU into a much more homogeneous body of labour organizations under Communist leadership. Although internal conflicts could not be avoided even under the new conditions, they were no longer based on fundamentally opposed views about the role of trade unions in society but instead on divergent national interests or on different interpretations of Communist ideology, or a combination of both. Notwithstanding the advantages of greater internal uniformity, the WFTU sought, especially from the mid-1950s on, to diversify its membership and to strengthen its claim to be the most representative international labour body. In pursuit of this objective it took to inviting both affiliated and nonaffiliated organizations to attend its world congresses, a tactic that achieved a certain amount of success especially with regard to labour organizations in less developed countries. And incidentally, seven world congresses have until now followed the founding congress in Paris in 1945: Milan (1949), Vienna (1953), Leipzig (1957), Moscow (1961), Warsaw (1965), Budapest (1969), Varna, Bulgaria (1973), and Prague (1978).

138. The headquarters of the WFTU were first established in Paris, but after the WFTU came apart in 1949 the French government declared it unwelcome on a charge of involvement in subversive activities. Thereupon in January 1951 the WFTU moved to the Soviet sector of Vienna. At this time Austria was still under four-power occupation and was in no position to resist the WFTU's presence, even though the Austrian trade union federation, the ÖGB, had been a charter member of the ICFTU. The peculiarities of this situation explain why the WFTU held its third world congress in Vienna, whereas since then all other congresses have taken place in Eastern Europe. Within a year of the restoration of Austria's sovereignty the government asked the WFTU to leave so that, as it explained, it could protect Austrian neutrality. In 1956 WFTU headquarters were moved to Prague where they have remained.

139. In 1950 the Stalin–Tito conflict, which occurred chiefly at governmental and party levels, spilled over into the labour sector and resulted in the expulsion of the Yugoslav national centre from the WFTU. Six years later it was invited to return at a time when the Soviet Union was seeking to normalize its relations with Yugoslavia. The Yugoslavs refused because of the decision of their Communist leadership to remain officially nonaligned, but since 1961 there have been Yugoslav observers at WFTU congresses.

140. In the first half of the 1960s the worsening of Sino-Soviet relations changed the posture of the WFTU's Chinese affiliate. This will be discussed in the chapter on the WFTU below. Another serious blow to the WFTU was the 1968 invasion of Czechoslovakia by the Warsaw Pact countries. The consequences of this action are also dealt with separately below. Other internal disagreements resulted from efforts by several affiliates, notably those in Italy and Rumania, to achieve greater independence within the WFTU. Such attempts were strongly resisted by the proponents of relatively tight centralization, led by the WFTU's largest and predominant affiliate, the All-Union Central Council of Trade Unions of the USSR. Because of the persistence of the minority and the embarrassment that would have been caused by their disaffiliation, a certain loosening up of discipline had to be conceded, but by comparison with the ICFTU the WFTU remains by far the more centralized organization.

141. Having for various reasons decided against the establishment of officially designated regional sub-units in the different areas of the world the WFTU instead opted during the 1960s for close relations and joint endeavors with independent or seemingly independent regional bodies in Latin America (CPUSTAL), Africa (AATUF), and the Middle East (ICATU). However, such ties were not intended to preclude a drive for WFTU affiliates in these areas, and a substantial portion of WFTU expenditures was actually channelled into organizing and related activities in the less developed areas. For this purpose, the links with the regional groupings provided the WFTU with an effective operating base and extensive contacts.

142. Just as the ICFTU adopted positions on virtually all major political and economic issues of the day, so did the WFTU, too, choose sides – and usually in opposition to the views of the ICFTU. That was certainly the case with regard to the Marshall Plan, the Schuman Plan, the European Defence Community, the Common Market, the North Atlantic Treaty Organization, West German rearmament, the Israeli-Arab conflict, and many other issues of major importance. But even in matters where on the surface the two internationals seemed to be of like views, as in their opposition to colonialism or racial discrimination, or in their support of peace and women's rights, the underlying rationale and the actions advocated to achieve their objectives were usually of an entirely different character.

143. The major goal of WFTU spokesmen and publications throughout the past two to three decades was world labour unity, and the principal targets were the ICFTU, the WCL, and their national affiliates. Although the goal remained well out of reach, the WFTU achieved a number of significant successes. These included the establishment of regularly scheduled meetings with WCL officials and a strikingly large number of criss-crossing bilateral relations between individual ICFTU and WFTU affiliates. These and other links within the international labour movements will be reviewed further on.

C. The Christian International: from CISC to WCL

144. In 1952 P. J. S. Serrarens retired as General Secretary of the CISC after 32 years of service. He was succeeded by Auguste Vanistendael who remained at the helm of the organization until 1967. Thus, for close to 50 years the Christian International had only two general secretaries. Such longevity in office plus the relative homogeneity of the CISC membership conferred on the top officials a substantial degree of authority. The change from Serrarens to Vanistendael signified more, however, than the mere passage of generations. It marked the beginning of a development that within a decade and a half was to transform the CISC into an entirely different type of organization. One aspect of this development was an advance into geographic areas previously not represented at all or only skimpily. The other was secularization.

145. At the 1952 congress in The Hague, the CISC counted 20 member organizations of which 12 were in Europe, six in Latin America, one in Asia, and the remaining one in Canada. (Other congresses held after 1952 took place in Antwerp in 1955, Vevey in 1958, Paris in 1961, Liège in 1964, Luxemburg in 1968, Geneva in 1969, Evian in 1973, and De Haan aan Zee in 1977.) Sixteen years later at the 1968 congress in Luxemburg the delegates represented 74 affiliates in 68 countries, including 29 in Latin America, 20 in Africa, 19 in Europe, five in Asia, and one in North America. To be sure, many and perhaps even most of the newly acquired organizations represented mere workers associations rather than trade unions, that is, minority groups and sections within established trade union bodies. Nevertheless the expansion was startling even if the actual membership count in 1968 was substantially less than the claimed figure of 12.7 million.

146. The new expansion into the Third World was the result of a deliberate policy decision, prepared over a period of several years, to channel CISC organizational resources to the less developed areas. In order to be successful, however, such a shift required a modification of the Christian articles of faith which had long served as the spiritual basis for the CISC. For the number of Buddhists, Moslems or Hindus who could be induced to join an explicitly Christian labour international was decidedly limited. The initial or intermediate solution was the adoption of a nonspecific interdenominationalism, as exemplified by the titles which the CISC conferred on its new regional organizations in Africa (the Pan-African Workers Congress, 1959), and Asia (the Brotherhood of Asian Trade Unionists, 1963). In Latin America, however, where Roman Catholicism was, and still is, the dominant faith, a specific reference to Christianity was retained by the CLASC (the Latin American Federation of Christian Trade Unions) from its founding in 1954 until 1971 when it changed its name to CLAT (the Latin American Workers Central). It should be noted, too, that a European Organization (EO) was founded in 1958, but it has since been dissolved and its members absorbed by the European Trade Union Confederation (see below).

147. The doctrinal universalization of the CISC was accompanied and reinforced by similar developments in those countries where the CISC had a majority of its dues-paying members – France, Belgium, Canada, and the Netherlands, and among these four especially France. In that country a prolonged struggle resulted in 1964 in the transformation of the former French Confederation of Christian Workers (CFTC) into the French Democratic Confederation of Labour (CFDT). Similar developments elsewhere led the CISC to drop from its 1964 action programme almost all mention of God, Christianity, and indeed any faith at all. At the 1968 congress in Luxemburg the last remaining references of a specifically Christian character were erased from the basic documents, though the preamble of the Declaration of Principles still referred to certain (non-denominational) spiritual values. The CISC itself emerged from this secularization process under the new name of the World Confederation of Labour (WCL). It also acquired at this time a new general secretary, Jean Brück, who was succeeded in 1976 by Jan Kulakowski.

148. In its newly adopted programme the WCL rejected the capitalist system and espoused the socialization of the means of production, democratic economic planning, and workers control. Thus, the organization which had come into being 50 years earlier as a centre of opposition to the socialist domination of international labour organizations had ended up by adopting the essence of its opponents' original programme.

Chapter IV. The International Confederation of Free Trade Unions

I. Organization and Structure

149. Among the three trade union internationals composed of national trade union federations the ICFTU is the most heterogeneous and most representative organization in geographic and ideological terms despite the loss of many African affiliates in the 1960s and the painful severance of the AFL-CI0 in 1969. Geographically it includes the largest national centre in every Western European country except France, Italy, and Belgium. It also covers a fair portion of Latin America and the Caribbean, still retains some affiliates in Africa, and has a respectable basis in those Asian countries that are not under Communist rule. In addition it includes Australia, New Zealand and the main body of Canadian unions. Ideologically its affiliates represent a broad range of views from which are excluded only trade unions under totalitarian direction, whether right or left. Accordingly, the ICFTU accommodates not only the unions of predominantly democratic and socialist orientation in Western Europe and other highly industrialized areas, but also the less conventional brands of socialism or collectivism encountered among unions in various Third World countries, the Christian socialist legacy of the Italian affiliate CISL, the Marxist socialism of the Guyana TUC, and the non-ideological business unionism of Canada and other countries.

150. A similar diversity characterizes the stage of social and economic development of the countries from which the ICFTU draws its members, and the same may be said of the independence of its members from external direction by governments. In other words, though many affiliates are reasonably free of control by governments (or political parties), the degree of their autonomy does vary considerably. It tends to be much greater in the more highly developed countries than in those still in the early stages of industrialization. As the constitution puts it, the ICFTU exists 'to unite the workers organized in the free and democratic trade unions of the world', but for purposes of determining eligibility for membership this principle must be regarded as an ideal rather than as a strict requirement.

A. Membership

151. The ICFTU constitution declares eligible for membership all bona fide national trade union centres that accept the aims and the constitution of the organization. There is no automatic bar to the affiliation of two or even more national centres from any one country. Affiliation is available even to individual unions. This, however, requires prior consultation with – and normally the approval of – an already affiliated national centre or centres, as well as of the International Trade Secretariat concerned. Final decision in all cases is up to the ICFTU Executive Board. There are a number of countries that are represented in the ICFTU by two or more affiliates. In 1975, for example, there were six each from Japan and Lebanon, four from Indonesia and Argentina, and three from Brazil and Pakistan. Dual membership from industrialized Western countries is less frequent but does occur, as for example in the cases of Sweden and Denmark where alongside the central body of manual workers unions the ICFTU also includes separate federations of white collar employees. Of course, without the consent of the principal federation such an arrangement would not be possible, as shown by the case of West Germany where the DGB has never consented to the ICFTU's acceptance of a separate white collar employees organization, the DAG.

152. Membership figures given out by international trade union bodies must be regarded with caution because they are subject to a certain amount of inflation. This is often the result of inaccurate reporting by affiliates which for reasons of prestige, particularly in competitive situations, are led to exaggerate their own strength. By and large, international organizations are compelled to accept the claims of their affiliates even if known to be inaccurate because it would be politically inexpedient to question them. The sobering effect of financial contributions calculated on the basis of membership reports does not operate in practice because it is precisely the organizations most prone to exuberant reporting which enter claims to large-scale forgiveness of their dues on grounds of inability to pay. Although the ICFTU thus has not been immune to exaggerated claims, nevertheless at least it furnishes more detailed and probably more trustworthy information on membership (and finances) than its rivals.

153. As the table below indicates, the ICFTU as of 1 January 1979, claimed 122 affiliates in 87 countries with a total membership of about 62,000,000. ('Real' membership is likely to be considerably less, if only dues-paying members are counted. The difference probably amounts to 10,000,000 if not more.)

154. It will be noted that between 1949 and 1962 the ICFTU experienced a significant increase in the number of countries represented and organizations affiliated. The number of individual members even continued to rise until 1969. Subsequently, however, a decline occurred in all categories. As regards countries and organizations, the decline was chiefly attributable to the departure of African affiliates that were acting for the most part under orders of their governments. The decline in actual membership was caused almost entirely by the disaffiliation of the AFL–CIO with a membership at the time of disaffiliation of almost 14,000,000. In the very recent past the membership figures have once again begun to increase.

ICFTU Membership Trends, 1949–1979

Year	Number of countries and territories	Number of organizations	Number of individual members represented by affiliates
1949	51	67	48,000,000
1951	59	76	50,500,000
1953	59	97	53,200,000
1955	75	109	54,300,000
1957	88	124	53,800,000
1959	97	137	56,000,000
1962	106	137	56,000,000
1965	96	121	60,300,000
1969	95	123	63,000,000
1972	91	115	48,600,000
1975	88	118	51,800,000
1979	87	122	67,000,000

155. The regional distribution of ICFTU membership for selected years is indicated in the table below. It reveals among other things the unbalancing effects of the American disaffiliation which left only the Canadian Labour Congress and the United Mine Workers in the North American category. The table also shows quite strikingly the corresponding increase in the relative importance of Western Europe, the remarkable growth of ICFTU affiliates in Asia, and the decimation of representation in Africa.

Percentage distribution of ICFTU membership by regions, selected years, 1949–1979

Region	1949	1955	1965	1975	1979
Europe	43.0	44.1	44.0	57.9	55.2
Africa	*	0.5	1.5	1.8	0.5
Asia	13.7	8.5	9.3	18.7	18.4
Near East	*	1.1	2.6	2.8	4.3
Oceania	*	1.9	1.7	3.2	3.3
North America	30.5	32.5	23.5	2.9	2.5
Latin America and Caribbean	12.3	11.4	17.4	12.7	15.8
	100.0	100.0	100.0	100.0	100.0

* means less than one-half of one percent

B. GOVERNING BODIES

156. The preponderance of European affiliates is to some extent reflected in the composition of the governing bodies of the ICFTU, although other factors besides membership – for example, geographic distribution – also determine the allocation of seats.

1. Congress

157. The supreme authority of the organization is its congress. It now meets at four-year intervals (they used to be shorter) to consider and decide on all major issues, including future activities, income and expenditures, and the election of the Executive Board and the General Secretary. Representation at the congresses is related directly to membership, but in a regressive proportion that is designed to prevent the very largest affiliates from completely eclipsing the smaller organizations. The International Trade Secretariats are entitled to be represented at congresses by non-voting delegates.

2. Executive Board

158. The trend toward longer intervals between meetings of the congress confirms the general rule that such bodies in large and loosely held together organizations like the ICFTU tend to be less significant in deciding major items than the smaller and more readily assembled executive bodies. The ICFTU constitution confers a large measure of authority on the Executive Board, including the right to act on behalf of the Confederation, to direct its activities, and to give effect to the decisions of the Congress. The Board consists of 29 elected members and, *ex officio*, the General Secretary as well as the President if the latter is not already an elected member. The International Trade Secretariats are represented by four non-voting members. As one would expect, the Board is widely representative in a geographic sense, in fact so much so that the weaker areas in terms of membership are greatly overrepresented, while the main centres of strength are correspondingly underrepresented. The line-up is indicated by the table on the next page.

159. Four seats in the North American category which used to be occupied by the AFL–CIO have been kept open for its eventual return. In addition to the 29 titular members of the Board there are 29 first substitutes and 29 second substitutes. This arrangement is intended not only to ensure that Board meetings will be fully attended but also to accommodate the easily frustrated ambitions of organizations and leaders aspiring to international honors and recognition. In this connection it should be noted that in addition to the largely honorific office of ICFTU president, which is filled by the Board and not by the Congress, the Constitution permits the designation of an unspecified number of vice-presidents. At present their number is 13.

Composition of the ICFTU executive board (elective members)

Region	Number of seats
Africa	3
Asia	5
Australia and New Zealand	1
Great Britain	2
Other countries of Europe	6
Latin America	3
West Indies	1
Middle East	2
North America	6
Total	29

3. Sub-Committee

160. As a rule the Executive Board has been meeting twice a year, though in certain years an extra meeting or two has had to be scheduled. Given the relatively large size of the Board and the consequent difficulty and expense of bringing its members together more frequently, the Constitution provides for a so-called Sub-Committee, composed of the President, the General Secretary, and nine members, plus one ITS representative, that can be consulted on questions of urgency or importance between Board meetings. Like the full Board, the Sub-Committee is representative of the ICFTU's geographic distribution, and for each seat there are again first and second substitutes.

4. Finance and General Purposes Committee

161. Although the Sub-Committee might have been envisaged by the framers of the Constitution as the inner core of the ICFTU's decision making procedure, that position is actually occupied by a different body, the Finance and General Purposes Committee. This group, technically also a subcommittee of the Board, emerged in 1968 from a consolidation of two predecessor groups: the Finance Sub-Committee and the International Solidarity Fund Committee. Its considerable powers are implied by its composition. Aside from the general secretary and the *ex officio* president, the six other voting members come exclusively from Western Europe, Asia, and Canada, and thus include the ICFTU's most important financial contributors. Two ITS representatives and the regional secretaries for Asia, Africa, and the Americas hold an associate membership which presumably means that they do not vote. The committee usually meets two or three times per year, and its regular agenda items include all key issues of resource allocation.

162. Major personnel decisions may also come under the group's jurisdiction. Thus, when in 1971 Harm Buiter's resignation created a vacancy in the general secretaryship, the Executive Board referred the matter of recommending a successor to the Finance and General Purposes Committee, it being understood that the committee's nominee, if endorsed by the Board, would be appointed on an acting basis until the next regular congress. (The constitution requires that the congress elect the general secretary.) In this particular instance the committee's unanimous choice, Otto Kersten of the German DGB, encountered a substantial amount of resistance in the Executive Board, particularly from its Asian, African and Latin American members. On a ballot vote at the Board's October 1971 meeting the nomination was referred back to committee for further consideration, as it was the hope of a number of Board members that their own choice, C. V. Devan Nair of Singapore, would be presented as an alternate nominee and then collect enough votes in the Executive Board. The committee, however, persisted in its original choice, and in January 1972 the full Board accepted its recommendation by a vote of 15 to 9 with one abstention, but only after the committee had warned that serious consequences would follow on rejection. Because the conflict so obviously engaged regional differences as well as large disparities in financial strength, it was in a sense a test of strength between the Executive Board whose membership, according to the British TUC, over the years had become increasingly weighted against the more substantial members and contributors and the Finance and General Purposes Committee with its European centre of gravity.

163. Later in the same year, that is 1972, another confrontation between European and non-European member organizations occurred in which the position upheld by the Europeans again carried the day. The occasion was the Tenth World Congress in London in July. The issue arose over the then impending founding of a European Trade Union Confederation (ETUC). It was the contention of the affiliates from Third World countries, backed up this time by unions from such non-European but industrialized countries as Canada and Australia, that if the European organization were to lack organic links with the ICFTU it would tend to preempt the resources and the loyalties of its affiliates at the expense of their much older ties to the world body. Under such circumstances, they argued, the ICFTU would become a greatly weakened organization, incapable of rendering assistance to those of its weaker affiliates that were sorely in need of it. The Europeans, however, rejected the demand for an explicit linkage of their new body with the ICFTU, patterned on the model of an associated regional organization like ORIT or ARO. They had already committed themselves to a type of European organization whose membership would be drawn from a wider circle than merely ICFTU affiliates, notably the Christian trade union organizations. Of course they did seek to reassure the non-European organizations that the establishment of the ETUC would have no adverse effects on their long-standing commitment to the work of the ICFTU, but it was exceedingly difficult to alleviate the concerns of the objectors.

164. In view of the foregoing events it is significant to note that on the occasion of the next following ICFTU congress, held in Mexico City in 1975, the Executive Board elected the first non-European ICFTU president. The position went to Dr. P. P. Narayanan of the Malaysian Trades Union Congress who thereby also became an *ex officio* member of the Finance and General Purposes Committee. At the same time C. V. Devan Nair of Singapore became an elected member. Thus for the first time unionists from the less developed countries joined the inner circle.

C. Secretariat

165. The secretariat of the ICFTU is headed by a general secretary who is elected by the congress but whose tenure under the constitution can be terminated either by the Executive Board or the Congress. During the difficult period which preceded the designation of the present holder of the office, Otto Kersten, the British suggested limiting the term of office to four years, that span being considered by them to be a long enough period to achieve an impact without generating opposition. The proposal failed to satisfy those Board members who objected that it would diminish the independence and effectiveness of the general secretary, and it was therefore not pressed.

166. Until 1972, the general secretary had invariably come from one of the smaller countries, in fact exclusively from Benelux. That choice was dictated in part by political considerations, namely the desirability of precluding big power rivalries and suspicions, and in part by technical considerations. For it so happens that the Benelux countries have always produced more than their relative share of people qualified to assume international trade union office in terms of linguistic skills, international outlook, talent for administration and negotiation and willingness to operate within the narrow constraints imposed by the often conflicting aims and expectations of an exceedingly heterogeneous membership.

167. The constitution confers on the Executive Board the right to appoint an indeterminate number of assistant general secretaries. At one time three positions at this rank were actually occupied and a fourth had been earmarked for occupancy, but in recent years only one assistant general secretary has held the office. The present incumbent is Jan Vanderveken, a Belgian national.

168. In the 1970s the number of staff members at ICFTU headquarters has varied from 70 to 75, about half of them at professional and technical level and half in secretarial and clerical positions. In 1962, by comparison, the headquarters staff amounted to 126 members. Of course, the contraction has been due to the severe financial stringencies of the past decade.

169 . ICFTU branch offices outside Brussels have been established mainly in cities where the organization has had to exercise a continuing liaison role, notably in Geneva at the International Labour Office and in New York City at the United Nations. Other branch offices were once located in Vienna, Tokyo, Beirut, Lagos and Addis Ababa, but the need to conserve funds has led to closings and reductions in staffing. Some 40 persons used to be employed either in branch offices or in ICFTU-financed educational institutions around the world, but that number has now been greatly reduced.

170. Recruitment and retention of top calibre personnel for staff positions are not easy tasks. The pool of potentially qualified persons for effective service at international trade union level is quite limited in almost any country. To have worked for an international trade union organization is only rarely considered to be an advantage for trade unionists who seek advancement in their own labour movement. Being away from one's home base may entail losing contact with influential constituencies and losing touch with important developments. Also, the material terms of employment offered by bodies like the ICFTU tend to be inferior to those held out by the intergovernmental agencies in Brussels, Paris, Luxemburg, Strassburg, Geneva, etc., and it clearly requires a good deal of idealism to be willing to forego them.

D. Finances

171. To finance its operations, the ICFTU has been relying for over twenty years on two principal sources of income: affiliation fees and voluntary contributions. The affiliation fees, which technically are required payments, go into the so-called General Fund from which all ordinary administrative and operational activities are to be paid. These include principally the costs of conferences and meetings, staff salaries, office expenses, and publications. On the other hand, the voluntary contributions are remitted to the so-called International Solidarity Fund (ISF) which mainly supports the regional activities of the ICFTU in the less developed areas, including the work of advisers and field representatives. The ISF is also used to subsidize regional ICFTU bodies and individual unions requiring external assistance and to help the International Trade Secretariats (nowadays only the International Federation of Plantation, Agricultural and Allied Workers) with their work in Asia, Africa, and Latin America.

172. For several years in the early 1960s, affiliation fees accounted for only about one-third of total ICFTU income, while voluntary contributions amounted to two-thirds. Fairly soon, however, the willingness of most affiliates to make sizable donations diminished sharply, largely because of disappointments over the slow pace of regional activities and the absence of dramatic successes. Currently the proportion of total income derived from affiliation fees amounts to two-thirds, so that in 1974, for example, out of approximately three million dollars taken in, two million came from obligatory affiliation fees and somewhat less than one million from special contributions.

173. Inflation has had, of course, the same impact on the ICFTU as on its constituents. Expenditures have risen at a faster rate than income. In addition, the ICFTU suffered a particularly severe financial blow when the AFL–CIO disaffiliated in 1969. Inevitably, affiliation fees have had to be raised quite regularly. They will amount to almost $80 per 1,000 affiliated members as of 1978. Most organizations in the less developed areas are unable to contribute at that rate, and some would not or could not contribute at almost any rate. It is thus not surprising to find that 66 organizations – more than half the total – benefited in 1974 from reductions granted by the Executive Board, with some reductions amounting to 100 per cent. However, the partially or wholly exempt group represents only about one-fourth of total membership.

174. The financial burden is a heavy one even for some organizations in industrialized countries, notably in those cases where the national central body receives a relatively small per capita contribution from its own affiliated unions. A fair example is the British TUC. For the TUC, the ICFTU affiliation fee constitutes about one-third of its own total income. Given such a high proportion and the financial sacrifice required to make it, it is understandable that the TUC has often been critical of ICFTU financial and accounting practices.

175. During the first half of the 1970s the demands on the ICFTU's General Fund became greater than could be met from current income, and the practice was begun of transferring a portion of ISF income to meet deficits in the General Fund. By 1975 these transfers had reached a point where they paid for about 25 per cent of all General Fund expenditures. This development served as a compelling reason for the adoption of a substantial increase in affiliation fees at the 1975 Congress in Mexico City.

176. The International Solidarity Fund will continue to depend on the willingness of a handful of organizations in the wealthier countries to contribute to the ICFTU beyond their fixed obligations. This group includes particularly the ICFTU affiliates in West Germany and Sweden, which together account for about 80 per cent of the income of the International Solidarity Fund, and to a lesser extent the Austrians, Canadians, Danes, Dutch, and Norwegians. The British TUC ceased to make voluntary payments some years ago because it did not have the means to do so.

E. Regional Organizations

177. The constitution adopted by the founding congress of the ICFTU in 1949 contained a provision mandating the establishment of regional organizations. This innovation in the structure of international labour organizations, vigorously urged at the time by the delegates from the United States and the less developed countries, was intended to accomplish two objectives. One was the avoidance of overconcentration of power at ICFTU headquarters; the other was the creation of a mechanism for dealing with problems distinctive to a particular region of the world. The preceding chapter contained an account of the implementation of the constitutional mandate in Europe, Asia, the Americas, and Africa. Although it is not possible to measure with any degree of accuracy the successful attainment of these objectives, it currently appears that at least with regard to the Western Hemisphere and Asia they have been reasonably well met. In both areas there is a regional organization – ORIT and ARO, respectively – which function as a limited power centre of its own and a channel for the development of the specific regional concerns of affiliates. Europe constitutes a special case because there the former regional organization of the ICFTU has been superseded by the establishment of an independent body whose ranks have a broader membership. Africa is also a special case because repeated efforts to form a lasting, even if not self-sufficient, regional body have failed to overcome the resistance of most governments to let their labour organizations maintain an international relationship.

178. To be sure, even in the relatively successful instances of Asia and the Americas there have been problems from time to time. To a substantial extent these may be attributed to the financial dependence of the regions on the centre, the efforts by the centre to require adherence to centrally set policies, occasional differences over personnel actions, and frequent attempts by the regions to safeguard the largest possible measure of autonomy. Consequently, when a regional organization reaches the stage of being able to assume responsibility for all or most of its financial requirements, that mark of progress tends to weaken the position of the central body. Recent trends in the case of both ICFTU regional organization – ARO and ORIT – confirm that observation, and though neither is by any means financially independent yet, they now function increasingly under their own direction.

1. ARO

179. The activities of ARO from 1973 to 1975 will serve to exemplify the special concerns of a regional organization. Besides holding a regularly scheduled regional conference of its affiliates, ARO organized during this time a special conference on unemployment, a joint meeting with Asian labour ministers (the fourth affair of its kind), a seminar on trade union research, and a conference on the state of the economy in Asian countries. These occasions helped affiliates to align their positions on subjects of area-wide concern, particularly problems of unemployment and the organization of agricultural workers, and to lobby national governments and international agencies on vital trade union concerns.

2. ORIT

180. In the Western Hemisphere the AFL–CIO has always played a key role in the affairs of ORIT, and its presence has generally been regarded as essential to the solvency and even the survival of the organization. From time to time, however, the weight of the North American colossus has caused antagonism among some Latin American unions which have feared a trade union variant of the Monroe Doctrine. It has also created concern at ICFTU headquarters which has blamed its clashes with the regional leadership on the protective umbrella held out over ORIT by the AFL–CIO. Given these circumstances, proposals have been floated from time to time to divide the Western Hemispheric organization into a Northern and a Southern part, but until the early 1970s they were not seriously pressed, if only because their implementation would have cost ORIT the 80 per cent portion of its budget contributed by the AFL–CIO (even more if one adds the Canadian contribution).

181. A new situation arose, however, when the AFL–CIO left the ICFTU. According to the letter of the ICFTU constitution that step should have simultaneously led to termination of AFL–CIO membership in ORIT. But none of the principal parties wanted to push the break to that consequential result. ORIT needed continued U.S. support, the ICFTU hoped for an early return of its American affiliate, and the AFL–CIO wanted to preserve its opportunities to influence the direction of trade union developments in Latin America. However, some European affiliates of the ICFTU, notably in the Scandinavian and Benelux countries, became increasingly dissatisfied with the irregularity of this arrangement. They also objected on ideological grounds to U.S. labour's influence in Latin America because they judged AFL–CIO regional activities to be too closely entwined with conservative business interests of local and U.S. origin and with dubious political objectives. A delegation of European trade union leaders and ICFTU officials visited several Latin American countries early in 1975 and came away with the impression that there was strong support among some important Latin American ICFTU affiliates for a North–South division. It later became clear, however, that this impression had been to some degree in error and that certainly neither the Mexican nor the Venezuelan national trade union centres, which are among the most influential in the area, were prepared to see the AFL–CIO leave ORIT. That ended the most recent effort at remaking ORIT into a purely Latin American organization. At subsequent ORIT congresses several important personnel changes in the regional secretariat were made for the purpose of improving the administrative and financial affairs of the organization. It now remains to be seen whether these changes, particularly the appointment of J. J. del Pino as ORIT general secretary, will lead to results that are satisfactory to all of the interested parties.

182. A substantial difference between ARO and ORIT stems from the fact that the former has no competition in its region, neither from a subsidiary of the other global trade union federations nor from an independent regional body, whereas ORIT has had to contend for many years with strong challenges from regional organizations of the World Confederation of Labour and the World Federation of Trade Unions. The WCL unit for Latin America, which since

1971 is known by the initials CLAT (Latin American Workers Center), appeals to a constituency that is not dissimilar from the membership and potential membership of ORIT. There is, however, a critical distinction. ORIT emphasizes gradual social reform, freedom from dogma, collective bargaining, and as far as possible non-political trade unionism. CLAT's philosophy seeks to combine a profound social revolution and the collectivization of the means of production with the maintenance of individual freedom and the political independence of workers' movements in (post-revolutionary) society. In the context of Latin America, the radicalism of CLAT's programme and the shrill tone of its propaganda have sometimes had the effect of placing ORIT on the defensive, especially on those occasions when ORIT has been vulnerable to accusations of associating with local oligarchies or with North American 'imperialism'. The truculence of CLAT has also had an important adverse effect on relations between ICFTU and WCL and has certainly antagonized the AFL–CIO beyond repair.

F. Publications

183. The principal official publication of the ICFTU is the bimonthly journal *Free Labour World*. It appears in the four official languages: English, French, Spanish, and German. Total circulation for all four editions is 10,000 copies. The *International Trade Union News* is a biweekly compilation of brief news items about the ICFTU itself, its affiliates, and events of general interest to trade unions. It, too, appears in the four official languages. The quarterly *Economic and Social Bulletin* reprints the full text of documents issued by the ICFTU and affiliates. In addition, the ICFTU produces occasional booklets and brochures of topical interest. Recent publications have dealt with workers' participation, trade union education, young workers, migrant workers, and apartheid. Mention must also be made of the separate publications of the ICFTU regional organizations, as represented for example by *Asian Labour*, the journal of the Asian Regional Organization.

II. Aims, Policies, and Activities

184. A diffuse international trade union organization like the ICFTU, composed of heterogeneous national centres that are themselves often a composite of individual unions with highly diverse outlooks on the proper role and aims of labour organizations, is bound to declare its objectives in terms broad enough to appeal to all segments of its members and potential members, and if possible without antagonizing them. For example, the participants in the founding of the ICFTU could readily agree on the rejection of all forms of totalitarianism. Yet they would not have been of one mind on the establishment of a socialist society as an explicit goal. Consequently the ICFTU statement of aims adopted in 1949 did not express any judgments on, or preferences for, particular social systems but concentrated instead on those aims to which trade unions almost everywhere – totalitarian systems excepted – could readily subscribe.

185. As shown below, some of the stated aims are directly related to an ongoing ICFTU activity and thus clearly within the control of the organization itself, for example the mandate to develop a programme of trade union and workers education, whereas others, like the establishment of full employment, reflect long-term objectives whose realization is beyond the reach of the ICFTU and its affiliates. They depend instead on the decisions of national governments and intergovernmental agencies.

A. Avowed Aims

186. 'The International Confederation of Free Trade Unions declares its aims to be:

a. to maintain and develop a powerful and effective international organisation at world-wide and regional levels, composed of free and democratic trade unions, independent of any external domination and pledged to the task of promoting the interests of working people throughout the world and of enhancing the dignity of labour;
b. to seek the universal recognition and application of the rights of trade union organisation;
c. to further the establishment, maintenance, and development of free trade unions, particularly in economically under-developed countries;
d. to weld international trade union solidarity by giving succour to the victims of all kinds of oppression, by giving token assistance to those suffering from the consequences of natural and industrial disasters and by providing support in all other cases where workers should stand shoulder to shoulder;
e. to undertake and coordinate the defence of the free trade unions against any campaign aiming at their destruction or at the restriction of their rights or at the infiltration and subjugation of labour organisations by totalitarian or other anti-labour forces;
f. to assist in providing peoples who have been victims of war and subjugation with all practicable means for the speedy rebuilding of their economies and in promoting international measures of aid for them, with full respect for their political and economic independence;
g. to strive for the establishment of full employment, the improvement of working conditions, the introduction, maintenance and extension of social security for all, and the raising of the standard of living of peoples of all countries of the world;
h. to encourage the development of the resources of all countries in order to further the economic, social and cultural progress of the peoples of the world, and particularly of economically under-developed countries and non-selfgoverning territories;
i. to advocate, with a view to raising the general level of prosperity, increased and properly planned economic cooperation among the nations in such a way

as will encourage the development of wider economic units and freer exchange of commodities and to seek full participation of workers' representatives in official bodies dealing with these questions;

j. to protect, maintain and expand the system of free labour and to eliminate forced labour everywhere;

k. to represent the free trade union movement in all international agencies which exist or may be set up to perform functions affecting the social and economic conditions of working people and to further the implementation of their decisions whenever desirable;

l. to establish and extend association with international organisations, both governmental and non-governmental, in work which will further the aims of the International Confederation of Free Trade Unions in protecting and advancing the interests of the peoples generally and guaranteeing human rights;

m. to support the establishment of a world system of collective security, but pending its attainment to further and support within the Charter of the United Nations all measures that are necessary for assuring the defence of world democracy and the freedom of nations against any totalitarian or imperialist aggression;

n. to carry out a programme of trade union and workers' education as a necessary adjunct to the Confederation's organisational activities in those countries where trade unions do not yet exist or are still weak and also as a means of promoting better understanding of the tasks of the free trade union movement everywhere;

o. to engage in and foster publicity work which will increase the knowledge and understanding of national and international problems confronting the workers, so as to enable them to make their struggle more efficacious and so as to realise the widest support for the Confederation's activities;

p. to maintain and develop an international clearing-house of information and research on the problems of trade union organisation, wages and working conditions, labour legislation, collective bargaining and any other matter related to the implementation of the Confederation's aims.'

B. General Activities

187. Most activities of international trade union organizations, other than the policy-making function, can be fitted into one of three sets of tasks: the representational work, the organizational work, and the service work. In practice one set will often be closely related to another so that it becomes difficult to distinguish them, but each contains certain central elements.

1. Representational Activities

188. The representational work consists essentially of two items:

1. presenting the organization's views before appropriate international agen-

cies and forums as an authoritative expression of labour's sentiments as a whole, or at least of a segment of organized labour, and then securing their incorporation into the conclusions and decisions of the agency concerned;

2. convincing national governments to construct their labour policies with due recognition to the existence of a body of internationally recognized standards and rights which they may not disregard with impunity.

Effective exercise of the representational tasks usually requires the use of publicity, lobbying techniques, mobilization of support, preparation of briefs and reports, and similar devices.

189. For the ICFTU with its worldwide terms of reference the relevant international agencies to be addressed have been the United Nations and virtually all of its specialized agencies, foremost of course the International Labour Organization, but including also UNESCO, the Food and Agricultural Organization, and others whose assigned areas of competence impinge on the ICFTU and its constituents. In addition, the ICFTU's regional organizations have their own links with intergovernmental bodies at regional level, such as the Economic Commissions for Europe, Africa, Latin America, and Asia.

190. In the International Labour Organization the tripartite system of representation ensures for trade unions and their international spokesmen an unparalleled opportunity for participation in decisions on issues of vital concern to them. The ILO has, therefore, always commanded a large share of the ICFTU's resources for representational (and service) tasks. Here it can express, directly and through its affiliated organization, a position on a wide range of social issues that are subject to international review and regulation, and it has at least a fair chance of affecting the final disposition in some vital way. Within the ILO's unique procedure for the international protection of trade union rights the ICFTU also can and does submit complaints against governments for violations of freedom of association and is assured at least of a hearing.

191. Of special importance in the ILO has been the ICFTU's effort in coordinating the work of the free trade unions at annual ILO conferences and in the Governing Body. Also, in the triennial elections for Governing Body membership the ICFTU has time and again succeeded in getting its own list of candidates for seats as worker members elected, even when its rivals, the WFTU and WCL, have made concerted efforts to promote a competitive slate.

192. The effective relationship which the ICFTU has established with the ILO is without parallel among other UN agencies. The consultative status accorded to nongovernmental organizations like the ICFTU by the UN Economic and Social Council and by the various specialized agencies is really more that of a tolerated outsider than that of a coequal participant. Moreover, as the ICFTU itself has pointed out, over the years the consultative status has suffered erosion not only from an increasing number of nongovernmental organizations to whom the same status has been all too readily extended but also from the fact that many governments which do not consult with trade unions in their own countries see no need to do so at the international level. Nevertheless, it is important for the ICFTU to be seen and heard at meetings of international agencies where it can take advantage of opportunities to advance its views on a wide range of issues, from the protection of human and trade union rights to the rules governing international trade. For to the extent that such matters as freedom of association, the creation of employment opportunities, the expansion of social services, the development of educational and training facilities and similar issues become legitimate subjects for international consideration, the ICFTU must steadily seek to influence the outcome in line with its proclaimed aims and the interests of its constituents.

2. Organizational Activities

193. The missionary or organizational tasks of the ICFTU are designed to promote and strengthen independent trade unionism in areas where it is weak or barely exists. They are carried out principally in Third World countries, but also include such European countries as Spain and Portugal. In view of the intimate ties between the ideology of a social system and the orientation of the trade unions and labour-management relations within that system, missionary activities are often highly competitive struggles between the ICFTU, WFTU, and to some extent the WCL. On the outcome may depend not only the future direction of a national trade union movement but also the fundamental social order of an entire country. Organizing activities may take various forms, but propagating the principles of free trade unionism is the most basic one. Subsidies for weak unions, paid study trips for selected leaders, and gifts of equipment such as office machines and vehicles are also included.

194. For structural, technical and political reasons the ICFTU has sometimes not been in the best position to support, much less to conduct, organizing work itself. In such cases it has left this task to the regional bodies and the International Trade Secretariats. The ITSs in particular are better able than the ICFTU to avoid identification with a political power bloc. The ITSs are also able to rely on their experience in dealing with economic and industrial issues that are specific to the industry for which they are competent, instead of having to depend mainly on a diffuse appeal based on the general merits of free and independent trade unionism.

195. A very substantial factor affecting the ICFTU's missionary work has been the proliferation of independent efforts under the direct aegis of ICFTU affiliates and former affiliates. Among present ICFTU members the largest sponsors of such activities – each conducted in a different way – are the West German DGB through the Friedrich-Ebert-Stiftung, the British TUC, the Israeli Histadrut, the Austrian ÖGB, the Swedish LO, and the Dutch FNV. Even larger than any of these operations, but now entirely outside the ICFTU, are the activities and institutes created by the AFL–CIO as its operating arms for Africa (the African–American Labor Center), Asia (the Asian–American Free Labor Institute), and Latin America (the American Institute for Free Labor Development).

196. Taken together, independent bilateral activities (independent because they take place beyond the ICFTU's area of direct control and bilateral because they often involve only two national organizations – the assistance-dispensing and assistance-receiving ones) have become a formidable element in international trade unionism, overshadowing, complementing, but to some extent also displacing the ICFTU's own missionary work. Independent actions are usually well financed, partly due to sizable government grants. Their technical apparatus is also of a high order. The existence of such initiatives constitutes a serious problem for the ICFTU because of the competitive challenge to one of its core activities and even more because of the possible dilution of loyalty toward the ICFTU that one must expect of unions which receive important assistance from a national rather than an international body. Unable to prevent the development and the expansion of bilateral activities, the ICFTU has asserted its competence to exercise at least a coordinating role, but this has neither high visibility nor is it easily discharged if the means and manpower are lacking. It should be noted, however, that ways have often been found to achieve practical cooperation in the field between national aid-dispensing institutes and the ICFTU's affiliates, its regional organizations, and the International Trade Secretariats, as for example in the form of jointly conducted programmes.

3. Service Activities

197. The third set of general tasks assumed by the ICFTU includes a range of service activities headed by education and training programmes, research, publicity, and technical assistance. In the educational area, for example, the ICFTU in one of its first major decisions founded an Asian Trade Union College in 1952. It is now located in New Delhi. Six years later it established an African Labour College in Uganda. In 1962 the ICFTU Inter-American Institute for Labor Studies was set up in Cuernavaca, Mexico. Subsequently the African operation had to be terminated because the Ugandan government decided to close the college, but the ICFTU continues to provide educational programmes in Africa on a decentralized basis. There has also been a change in the status of the Latin American institution. It has recently been transferred to the ICFTU's Mexican affiliate, the CTM, for its primary use but will be available to the ICFTU and its affiliates in the region. Similarly, the Asian Trade Union College has also changed its character and purpose. Thus, in Asia and Latin America as well as in Africa the emphasis is now on decentralized educational activities. Obviously they represent less of a drain on ICFTU resources.

198. The service activities are closely related to the organizing and representational tasks and in fact derive their justification from that link. Education and training programmes are therefore never an end in themselves but are intended to improve the technical ability of union leaders and staff officials to carry out their day-to-day responsibilities, and at the same time to raise their understanding of the free trade union principles for which the ICFTU is the exponent. In the same way the research work is not 'pure' research, but is designed to bolster the ICFTU's advocacy of a particular cause, whether it is a question of tariff reductions, shortcomings in the observance of minimum wage legislation, protection of migrant workers, or international monetary policy.

C. Policy Issues

199. It is not possible to indicate even approximately all the issues on which, over the years, the ICFTU has taken a position. Such a list would be far too large. It would include, to begin with, many items of obvious and direct concern to an international trade union body, such as freedom of association, problems of employment and unemployment, industrial democracy, the rights of migrant workers, and social insurance. Beyond such items one would also have to include a host of issues of a political and ideological nature on which the ICFTU has felt compelled to express a position because they make up the vital context in which trade unions must operate. These would include violations of human and trade union rights, the legitimacy (or illegitimacy) of particular political regimes, as well as specific government actions, questions affecting world peace and rearmament, the creation of supranational bodies such as the European Economic Community, and many others.

200. ICFTU pronouncements on policy issues are not limited to the resolutions adopted by congresses but also emerge from the more frequent meetings of executive bodies. In addition they are to be found regularly in the editorials of *Free Labour World*, the official journal, and are to some extent implicit in the content of this and other official publications.

201. Illustrative of the breadth of concerns is the list of resolutions adopted by the Madrid Congress in 1979. It included considered expressions of views on individual countries, entire regions, international institutions, and widespread problems:

1. Namibia
2. Ethiopia
3. Iran
4. Zimbabwe
5. Latin America
6. Chile
7. Argentina
8. Nicaragua
9. Tunisia
10. Cyprus

11. Middle East
12. Indo-China
13. Transnational corporations
14. The International Labor Organization
15. The International Monetary Fund
16. The World Economic Summit Meeting
17. The International Year of the Child
18. International aid in natural disasters
19. Trade union rights of public employees
20. Government interference with trade unions rights
21. Peace and disarmament
22. Human rights
23. Women and trade unions

202. The actual positions taken, the strictures expressed (if any), and the recommendations advocated are usually predictable from the general principles for which the ICFTU stands. There is a strong tendency to select issues which tend to unite the constituent organizations and to overlook those that are likely to be divisive even if meritorious. For example, although the state of emergency imposed on India under the rule of Indira Gandhi severely circumscribed the exercise of political rights throughout the country and the freedom of action of Indian unions, and though it led to the imprisonment of a substantial number of union leaders, the ICFTU at no time issued a public protest. Any attempt to do so would have encountered opposition from ICFTU affiliates in India and probably other parts of Asia because, up to a point, their views of the imposed emergency were more sympathetic than hostile. For the ICFTU the practical even if not the noble solution was to make discreet representations to the Indian government.

203. When it becomes impossible to avoid an issue that is controversial, as may occur for example when an influential affiliate insists on its consideration, an effort can still be made to negotiate a compromise and to formulate the resolution or policy statement in terms that elicit unanimity or something close to it. Only infrequently does such an attempt fail, for international trade union bodies, like their constituents at national level, place a high premium on the appearance of complete harmony and deprecate divisions of opinion. The rare failures to reach unanimity are almost inevitably the result of a clash of national interests or of strong political engagements. One such instance occurred at the Mexico City Congress in 1975 over a resolution on Portugal. On this occasion a minority led by the British TUC and joined by the ICFTU's affiliates in Belgium and Finland fought against, and ultimately refused to endorse, a statement that contained a provision condemning Portuguese political forces motivated by dictatorial ideologies that were seeking to control the trade unions for their own purposes. They objected in particular to language that would offend the country's principal labour federation, which is dominated by the Communists. It should be stressed, however, that such differences, or at least their outward expressions, are far more often the exception than the rule.

III. Relations with Other Organizations

A. The International Trade Secretariats

204. In the network of international trade union bodies the quality of the relationship between organizations can be of great importance. For the ICFTU the most significant external links have always been its relations with the autonomous International Trade Secretariats as a collective entity and as individual and independent organizations. The activities of the ITSs deserve a separate chapter, but their ties to the ICFTU can best be discussed in the present context.

205. The basic document governing ICFTU–ITS relations is the revised Milan Agreement of 1951, as approved by the General Conference of the ITSs in 1966 and 1967 and as ratified by the ICFTU Congress in 1969. That document, which resembles a treaty between sovereign powers, defines the terms of relationships by means of the following provisions:

1. The ICFTU recognizes the autonomy of the ITSs and likewise recognizes the General Conference of the ITSs as their collective body but reserves the right to engage in individual relations with any single ITS.
2. The contracting parties explicitly recognize that they are in fact part of the same international trade union movement and that such recognition implies ITS adoption of the general policy of the ICFTU. They pledge themselves to cooperate in all matters of common interest.
3. The parties specify in considerable detail their rights to reciprocal representation in the congresses and executive body meetings of their respective organizations.

206. This formal agreement is, of course, only a bare outline that does not even begin to reflect the close and manifold relationships that have evolved in practice, even if not always without friction. There are, to begin with, the almost daily contacts between members of the ICFTU secretariat and their counterparts in the ITSs on issues of common interest. Then there are the more formal joint meetings convened from time to time to consider the problems confronting ICFTU/ITS operations in particular countries or regions, or in connection with particular topics, for example the joint working party on multinational companies. The practice has also grown up of holding informal ICFTU/ITS meetings at secretariat level before sessions of the ICFTU Executive Board. And of far from negligible importance is the fact that both sides have recruited persons from each other's ranks to fill vacancies in top level positions. Over the years several ICFTU general secretaries and assistant general secretaries have come out of the ITSs, and presently the top officials of several ITSs once held responsible posts in the ICFTU.

207. The underlying reason for the character of the relationship is close at hand. The ITSs consist in overwhelming proportion of the same individual unions that indirectly constitute the ICFTU – indirectly because the affiliation to the ICFTU is almost invariably through the national centre. There are, however, some important exceptions on both sides of the ledger. ITS membership does include some unions whose national centre is not affiliated with the ICFTU. By the same token, the national centres affiliated with the ICFTU often have in their ranks certain unions that have chosen not to belong to the ITS for their particular industrial sector. Occasionally these exceptions can assume great importance. For example, despite the AFL–CIO's exit from the ICFTU in 1969 individual AFL–CIO unions retained their ITS affiliation. In fact they were encouraged by the AFL-CIO to do so as a way of maintaining a vital link between American labour and the international labour movement.

208. That there are tangible advantages both for the ICFTU and the ITSs in regarding themselves as part of the same movement emerges from the fact that some ITS have been able to enrol individual unions in countries where the government has prohibited the national centre from belonging to the ICFTU. The fine distinction is presumably based on the assumption that ICFTU membership would signify a political or ideological commitment to which certain non-aligned governments object, whereas ITS membership appears to them to signify an acceptable expression of purely economic, i.e. nonpolitical, solidarity. Logically, of course, this differentiation makes no sense in view of the terms of the compact between the ICFTU and the ITSs, as indicated above, but logic does not necessarily dictate government policy.

209. Significant differences between ICFTU and ITSs over membership criteria have arisen only where there has been an important ideological element. When the International Graphical Federation (IGF) insisted on admitting a printing industry union affiliated with the Communist-directed French CGT, which belongs to the World Federation of Trade Unions, the ICFTU broke off relations with the IGF. It ought to be noted, however, that whereas the action of the IGF clearly contravened the ICFTU–ITS compact, it also demonstrated the dependence of that compact on voluntary adherence. In other words, the ITSs are genuinely autonomous organizations and not subordinate to the ICFTU.

210. So as to meet the ICFTU on reasonably even terms whenever practical problems of mutual interest need to be resolved, the ITSs have generally preferred to deal collectively with the ICFTU through a coordinating and liaison body under their own control. At present their agency is the General Conference of the ITSs. It holds annual meetings at which problems common to the ITSs are reviewed and representatives to ICFTU executive bodies designated. (The ICFTU is represented at the general conference of the ITSs by top officials.) Given their own somewhat divergent interests and constituencies, and given further the inevitable differences in the personalities and outlooks of leading officials, the ITSs are rarely able to achieve complete unanimity.

B. World Confederation of Labour

211. The existence of two international trade union federations – ICFTU and WCL – with similar and sometimes even identical views on many basic issues has frequently called into question the terms of their relationship and the possibility of a merger. The prospect of unification became particularly acute after the WCL in 1968 shed its specific Christian identity, but it is doubtful whether that objective is much closer now than it was ten years ago.

212. In 1974 the executive bodies of both organizations approved the creation of a joint ICFTU/WCL Working Committee, composed of high level officials, 'to study the means for developing further cooperation between the two internationals and to seek ways and means for unification'. However, the only tangible result of this most recent effort was the strengthening of joint work in various international agencies, and the further development of common approaches toward the struggle against apartheid, multinational companies, and such other issues as migrant workers. The fact that the European affiliates of ICFTU and WCL now belong to a single organization at European level, namely the European Trade Union Confederation, has also been a positive element but not sufficient yet to change the basically distant character of ICFTU–WCL relations at worldwide level.

213. On the negative side, the antagonisms between the ICFTU's and WCL's regional organizations in Latin America have hardly become less bitter. Also, the relatively recent appointment of a new WCL general secretary has seemingly strengthened rather than weakened the resolve of that organization to maintain a separate existence in spite of pressure from some of its important constituents to make every effort to reach a satisfactory understanding with the ICFTU. Given the enormous disparity in size and resources between the two organizations, it may well be that any negotiations aimed at merger will always appear to some key personalities on the WCL side as a crude take-over effort in which the smaller side will ultimately disappear without a trace. Such reflections, whether valid or not, are perhaps a greater obstacle to unity than the difficulty of working out the vexing problems of administration and personnel that always accompany merger talks between labour organizations.

C. World Federation of Trade Unions

214. In the management of the ICFTU's external affairs, the most complex problem for some time now has been the effort to retain control over the posture toward the WFTU. Among the many elements impinging on that effort two have been of special importance: the unceasing challenge from the WFTU and the lack of cohesiveness among the ICFTU's own affiliates about the proper course of action.

215. There are several dimensions to the WFTU challenge. Competitive organizing in Third World countries is one, and though WFTU successes have not been overwhelming, there is no question that the drives are multiplying. It is also possible that their quality is improving. Equally significant have been the WFTU's attempts to seize a kind of moral leadership on such sensitive issues as apartheid, multinational companies, nuclear testing and controls, peace and disarmament, unemployment, and others that easily lend themselves to propagandistic exploitation. Usually these campaigns have been accompanied by appeals to the ICFTU for world labour unity, solidarity, common action, joint manifestos, demonstrations, and other variants of making common cause. Although the ICFTU has consistently rejected these overtures, the WFTU has not allowed itself to become discouraged. Evidently the potential rewards are worth persistent effort. Western recognition of the legitimacy of labour organizations in the Soviet bloc – and of the WFTU – has been a long-sought aim, for it would imply an acknowledgement of a key principle, namely that the role and the tasks of trade unions in capitalist and socialist societies are fundamentally and justly different, and that therefore they cannot be judged by the same criteria, whether in relation to freedom of association, independence from party and government controls, or bargaining autonomy.

216. Rising differences within the ICFTU's own camp over the appropriate response to the WFTU have made adherence to a consistent policy a difficult undertaking. An especially bothersome element has been the fact that a large number of ICFTU affiliates have for over a decade now maintained bilateral contacts with individual WFTU affiliates in Eastern Europe despite a long-standing ICFTU policy of advising against them. A first concerted ICFTU attempt in 1967 to bring the straying affiliates back into the fold by appointing a committee to examine the whole range of East–West trade union contacts failed to solve the contradiction between ICFTU policy on one hand and the autonomy of affiliates on the other. That failure contributed heavily to the disaffiliation of the AFL–CIO in 1969. A second ICFTU effort was launched in 1973 by reactivating the 1967 committee. Its subsequent report upheld the ICFTU's refusal to enter into 'any relationship with international or regional bodies whose policies are in diametrical conflict with free and democratic trade union objectives', but it also conceded that in the area of bilateral East–West contacts each national centre had to take its decision in the light of its own circumstances. The report characterized the purpose of the WFTU's world labour unity campaign as a way of serving Soviet foreign policy aims and warned that divisions in the ICFTU's ranks would surely be exploited by the other side. Nevertheless, it was apparently compelled by the reality of the enormous number of East–West trade union exchanges to express impartial respect for the motives both of those ICFTU affiliates who do make visits to Communist bloc countries and those who do not.

217. The failure to condemn the contacts foreshadowed an escalation of East–West ties from bilateral to multilateral levels. This occurred in 1974 when, within the framework of the Second European Conference of the

International Labour Organization, an informal consultative meeting of trade unions from Western and Eastern Europe took place in Geneva. It was the first time since the 1949 split in the WFTU that representatives of all the various national centres had sat down together. To avoid any misunderstanding about its own part in the affair the ICFTU took pains to emphasize that neither it nor the WFTU had been represented at the meeting. (However, their two general secretaries did meet informally on this occasion.) Multilateral meetings at European level between ICFTU, WFTU, and WCL affiliates were held again in 1975 and 1977 to discuss the work environment, the use of dangerous substances and products in industry, and trade union education and training. A further conference is envisaged for 1979.

218. Multilateral meetings involving ICFTU, WFTU, and WCL representatives have also been held on several occasions under UN auspices. The most recent such meeting in Geneva in July 1977 brought together top officials of the three trade union confederations and high-level functionaries of the UN and several of its specialized agencies. The items on the agenda included unemployment, inflation, progress toward a new international economic order, and the preparation of codes of conduct to control the activities of multinational companies.

219. Whether officially represented or not at such meetings, the ICFTU has by no means been able to overlook their repercussions on the cohesion and uniformity of attitudes among its own affiliates. It has also had to give some weight to the fact that for the last few years its largest affiliate, the British TUC, has almost routinely adopted resolutions at its own annual congresses urging a rapprochement between ICFTU and WFTU. The ICFTU is compelled, therefore, to tread a narrow path. On one hand it must heed the imperative of preserving intact its character as the international embodiment of free and democratic trade unions. To veer too far away from that would erode its credibility, alienate important affiliates, and last but not least cut all hope of ever regaining the AFL-CIO as a member. On the other hand, it cannot simply rebuff or even ignore the supporters in its ranks of step-by-step East–West trade union rapprochements, especially when the supporters act in consonance with the foreign policies of their own governments. Recently the ICFTU Executive Board called on its affiliates to avoid in their international contacts any initiatives that might directly or indirectly weaken the ICFTU and the principles for which it stands, and to confine their multilateral contacts with unions in Communist and non-aligned countries to activities conducted within an ILO framework. It is uncertain whether these policy guidelines are a satisfactory response to the general problem, but if for the time being they are the best that can be obtained it still remains to be seen whether they can command general acceptance.

List of ICFTU affiliated organizations (as of 1 January 1979)

Country	Organization	Membership 1/1/1979
Argentina	Confederación General del Trabajo de la República Argentina (CGT)	500,100*
Australia	Australian Council of Trade Unions	1,800,000*
Austria	Oesterreichischer Gewerkschaftsbund	1,628,803
Bangladesh	Jatio Shramik League	1,200,000*
Barbados	Barbados Workers' Union	15,000
Basque Country	Solidaridad de Trabajadores Vascos (in exile)	100,000
Belgium	Fédération Générale du Travail de Belgique	900,000*
Belize (former British Honduras)	The General Workers' Development Union	3,000*
Bermuda	Bermuda Industrial Union	5,207
Bolivia	Federación Nacional de Trabajadores de Comercio, Empleados de Industria y Ramas Anexas	6,154*
Brazil	Confederaçâo Nacional dos Trabalhadores no Comercio (National Confederation of Commercial Workers)	2,500,000*
	Confederaçâo Nacional dos Trabalhadores em Transportes Terrestres (National Confederation of Road Transport Workers)	500,000*
	Confederaçâo Nacional dos Trabalhadores em Comunicaçôes e Publicidade (National Confederation of Communication and Publicity Workers)	65,000*
Canada	Canadian Labour Congress	1,300,000*
Chile	Federación Nacional de Sindicatos de la Industria Azucarera (FENAZU)	7,153*
China	Chinese Federation of Labour	400,000*
Colombia	Confederación de Trabajadores de Colombia	1,200,000*
	Unión de Trabajadores de Colombia	1,878,000
Costa Rica	Confederación Costarricense de Trabajadores Democraticos	12,000*
Curaçâo	Algemeen Verbond van Vakverenigingen – Curaçâo (General Federation of Trade Unions – Curaçâo)	12,975*
Cyprus	Cyprus Workers' Confederation (SEK)	32,629*
	Cyprus Turkish Trade Unions Federation (Türk-Sen)	10,069

Country	Organization	Membership 1/1/1979
Denmark	Landsorganisationen i Danmark (Danish Federation of Trade Unions)	1,046,000*
	Faellersrådet for danske Tjenestemandsog Funktionaerorganisationer (FTF) (Federation of Danish Civil Servants and Salaried Employees Organisations)	251,500
Dominica	Dominica Trade Union	520*
Dominican Republic	Confederación Nacional de Trabajadores Dominicanos (CNTD)	49,450*
Ecuador	Confederación Ecuatoriana de Organizaciones Sindicales Libres	80,000*
El Salvador	Confederación General de Sindicatos	38,000*
Estonia	Eesti Meremeeste Union (in exile) (Estonion Seamen's Union (in exile)	203*
Ethiopia	Confederation of Ethiopian Labour Unions	28,000*
Falkland Islands	Falkland Islands General Employees' Union	400*
Fiji	Fiji Trades Union Congress	30,000*
Finland	Suomen Ammattiliittojen Keskusjärjestö (SAK) (Central Organisation of Finnish Trade Unions)	951,190*
	Toimihenkilö-ja Virkamiesjärjestöjen Keskusliitto (TVK) (Confederation of Salaried Employees in Finland)	261,733
France	Confédération Générale du Travail – Force Ouvrière	905,000*
Gambia	Gambia General Workers' Union	3,002*
Germany (Fed. Republic)	Deutscher Gewerkschaftsbund	7,751,523*
Great Britain	Trades Union Congress	11,865,390
Greece	Greek General Confederation of Labour (GSEE)	300,000*
Grenada	Grenada Trade Union Council	3,000*
Guatemala	Central de Trabajadores Federados	15,000*
Guyana	Guyana Trades Union Congress	50,000*
Honduras	Confederación de Trabajadores de Honduras	35,000*
Hong Kong	Hong Kong and Kowloon Trades Union Council	85,000*
Iceland	Althydusamband Islands (Icelandic Federation of Labour)	42,402
	Bandalag starfsmanna rikis og baeja (BSRB) (Federation of State and Municipal Workers)	12,134*

Country	Organization	Membership 1/1/1979
India	Hind Mazdoor Sabha (Workers' Federation of India)	2,100,000
	Indian National Trade Union Congress	3,209,380
Indonesia	Kongres Buruh Islam Merdeka (KBIM) (Free Islamic Trade Union Congress)	130,000*
	Gabungan Serikat Buruh Islam Indonesia (GASBIINDO) (Federation of Indonesian Islamic Trade Unions)	110,000
	Gerakan Organisasi Buruh Sjarikat Islam Indonesia (GOBSI) (Federation of Sjarikat Islam Trade Unions)	50,000*
	Sarikat Buruh Muslimin Indonesia (SARBUMUSI) (Federation of Indonesian Moslem Trade Unions)	100,000*
Israel	General Federation of Labour in Eretz-Israel (HISTADRUT)	800,000
Italy	Confederazione Italiana Sindacati Lavoratori (Italian Confederation of Workers Trade Unions)	2,100,000*
	Unione Italiana del Lavoro (Italian Federation of Labour)	800,000*
Jamaica	National Workers' Union of Jamaica	21,056*
	Bustamante Industrial Trade Union	130,368*
Japan	Japan Coalminers' Union (TANRO)	15,000*
	All Japan Federation of Metal Miners' Unions (ZENKO)	9,000*
	All Japan Federation of Municipal Traffic Workers' Unions (TOSHIKO)	20,000
	Japan Postal Workers' Union (ZENTEI)	190,000
	Japan Broadcast Corporation Workers' Union (NIPPORO)	7,700*
	Japanese Confederation of Labour (DOMEI)	1,400,000
	Japan Telecommunications Workers' Union (ZENDENTSU)	270,000
Korea	Federation of Korean Trade Unions	466,812
Lebanon	Ligue des Syndicats des Employés et des Ouvriers dans la République libanaise	13,000*
	Fédération des Syndicats-Unis des Employés et Ouvriers au Liban	10,000*
	Fédération ouvrière des Offices autonomes et des Entreprises publiques et privées au Liban	3,617*

Country	Organization	Membership 1/1/1979
	Federation of Petroleum Trade Unions in Lebanon	1,923*
	Fédération des Syndicats des Employés des Banques au Liban	5,000*
	Federation of Insurance Sector Employees in Lebanon	1,000*
	Fédération des Syndicats des Employés du Commerce au Liban	1,000*
	Federation of Syndicates of Health and Education Sector in Lebanon	5,000*
	Workers' Syndicates Federation of Sea Transport in Lebanon	8,000*
	Federation of Airlines Companies Employees and Labours of Lebanon	3,800*
Lesotho	Basutoland Federation of Labour	12,000
	Lesotho Council of Workers	3,000
Liberia	Liberia Federation of Trade Unions	10,000
Luxembourg	Confédération Général du Travail du Luxembourg	32,000*
Malagasy Republic	Fivondronamben 'ny Mpiasa Malagasy (FMM) (Confederation of Workers of the Malagasy Republic)	8,000*
Malawi	Trades Union Congress of Malawi	6,000*
Malaysia	Malaysian Trades Union Congress	255,000*
Malta	General Workers' Union	27,000
Mauritius	Mauritius Labour Congress	36,260*
Mexico	Confederación de Trabajadores de Mexico	1,000,000*
Netherlands	Nederlands Verbond van Vakverenigingen (Netherlands Federation of Trade Unions)	724,000*
New Zealand	New Zealand Federation of Labour	220,000*
Nicaragua	Confederación de Unificación Sindical	1,500*
Nigeria	United Labour Congress of Nigeria	
Norway	Landsorganisasjonen i Norge (Norwegian Federation of Trade Unions)	680,000
Pakistan	Pakistan National Federation of Trade Unions	100,000*
	All-Pakistan Federation of Labour	363,000*
	All-Pakistan Federation of Trade Unions	295,550*
Panama	Confederación de Trabajadores de la República de Panamá	1,000*
Papua New Guinea	Papua New Guinea Trade Union Congress	14,800*
Paraguay	Confederación Paraguaya de Trabajadores	15,000*
Peru	Confederación de Trabajadores del Peru	480,000
	Confederación Nacional de Trabajadores	120,000

Country	Organization	Membership 1/1/1979
Philippines	Trade Union Congress of the Philippines	350,000*
Puerto Rico	Federación Libre de los Trabajadores de Puerto Rico	105,000*
	Federación del Trabajo del Puerto Rico	80,000*
St. Helena	St. Helena General Workers' Union	685*
St. Kitts-Nevis	St. Kitts-Nevis Trades and Labour Union	2,743*
St. Lucia	St. Lucia Seamen and Waterfront Workers' Trade Union	600*
	St. Lucia Workers' Union	2,000*
St. Vincent	St. Vincent Federated Industrial and Agricultural Workers' Union	2,000*
San Marino	Confederazione Generale Democratica dei Lavoratori Sammarinesi (General Democratic Confederation of Workers of San Marino)	1,782*
Seychelles	National Workers' Union (Seychelles)	6,000
Sierra Leone	Sierra Leone Labour Congress	40,000*
Singapore	National Trades Union Congress	150,000
Spain	Unión General de Trabajadores	250,000
Sri Lanka	Ceylon Workers' Congress	125,000
Surinam	Algemeen Verbond van Vakverenigingen in Suriname 'De Moederbond' (General Federation of Trade Unions in Surinam 'De Moederbond')	7,000*
Sweden	Landsorganisationen i Sverige (Swedish Confederation of Trade Unions)	2,057,290
	Tjänstemännens Centralorganisation (Swedish Central Organisation of Salaried Employees)	991,216
Switzerland	Schweizerischer Gewerkschaftsbund	468,508*
Trinidad	Trinidad and Tobago Labour Congress	50,000*
Tunisia	Union Générale Tunisienne du Travail	175,000*
Turkey	Türkiye Isçi Sendikalari Konfederasyonu (Türk-Is) (Turkish Confederation of Trade Unions)	1,800,000
United States	United Mine Workers of America	278,462
Upper Volta	Organisation Voltaïque des Syndicats Libres	6,000*
Uruguay	Confederación General de Trabajadores del Uruguay	50,000*
Venezuela	Confederación de Trabajadores de Venezuela	700,000*

* Figures relate to an earlier date of count

Chapter V. World Federation of Trade Unions

I. Organization and Structure

220. The World Federation of Trade Unions (WFTU) is an international organization whose core membership consists of national labour federations in countries governed by Marxist-Leninist parties, thus mainly the Soviet Union, Eastern Europe, Cuba and a few others. It also counts among its adherents a number of labour organizations in non-Communist countries. In terms of total membership the WFTU is the largest international labour federation with a claimed 190 million individual members as of 1978. By far the biggest contingent is represented by the central labour body of the Soviet Union (AUCCTU) which by itself accounts for almost two-thirds of the total. The weight and influence of that one organization, taken in conjunction with the dominant position of the Soviet Union in the political community of Communist countries, have kept the WFTU closely tied to the pursuit of Soviet foreign policy objectives in the various areas of the world.

A. Membership

221. The WFTU claims to be the most representative international labour federation. A detailed breakdown of its membership by regions or by country has not been made public since the exodus of Western unions in 1949. However, WFTU congresses usually release aggregate figures. They are presented in the table on the following page.

222. Several clarifications are necessary. First, the figure for January 1949 still includes the free trade unions which were just then on the point of leaving the WFTU. The only slightly lower figure for July 1949 purports to show the state of the membership soon after their departure, as given at the Milan WFTU World Congress. Yet when the disaffiliated unions set up the International Confederation of Free Trade Unions (ICFTU) at the end of 1949, they claimed an initial total membership of 49 million, mostly derived from former WFTU affiliates. (Only two important organizations in the new ICFTU – the American Federation of Labor and the West German DGB – had not previously been part of the WFTU.) It would appear, therefore, that the WFTU recouped almost its entire membership loss of at least 30 million in a mere six months – an almost miraculous feat. Even the hasty admission of several organizations whose applications for membership had previously been

WFTU membership and affiliated national centers, 1949–1978

Year	Membership of affiliated organizations	Number of affiliated national centers
1949 (January)	76,100,000	
1949 (July)	71,800,000	47
1953	80,400,000	
1957	92,600,000	
1961	119,500,000	39
1965	139,900,000	
1969	n.a.	51
1973	151,000,000	55
1975	180,000,000	74
1978	190,000,000	73

opposed by Western trade union leaders (because they feared that their entry would strengthen the WFTU's Communist wing) cannot entirely account for such a remarkable recovery. It seems likely, therefore, that for prestige reasons some generous adjustments were made in the actual membership figures of WFTU affiliates for 1949.

223. Second, already before the 1949 split the bulk of WFTU membership was located in countries under Communist-led governments. This has continued to be the case. Allowing for certain inter-county differences, these unions generally operate under close guidance provided by the ruling Communist parties. Having no significant bargaining functions and exercising only a modest claims-making and protective role, they would have little to do – outside of their major production-raising tasks – if they were not also involved quite heavily in administering the national social insurance system and rest, recreation, and welfare programmes. Union involvement in these programmes is indeed the chief inducement for taking out union membership, for nonmembership could lead to serious disadvantages. As a result, the extent of union membership, even if technically not compulsory, is in practice almost coextensive with the total industrial labour force. The huge numbers thus produced help to account for the fact that the total proportion of WFTU membership derived from unions in Communist countries alone amounts to over 90 per cent.

224. Third, the membership claims of all WFTU affiliates, even those in non-Communist countries, are difficult to verify. The latter include the relatively large Communist-led federations in France and India, and a number of smaller organizations in some twenty-five to thirty other countries. (The Italian affiliate, CGIL, withdrew in 1978.) Because the labour movements in some of these countries are often split among several rival organizations, they are usually induced by domestic competitive considerations to inflate their membership claims. That practice is of course not unique to WFTU affiliates.

225. Fourth, the membership figures for 1969 are not available although a congress was held that year. This is probably due to the fact that China and Indonesia, which had previously been among the major WFTU affiliates, did not attend the 1969 World Congress. Had there been a published membership count, it would probably have shown a decline – a fact which the WFTU leadership was apparently unwilling to admit. The substitute figure actually released, which included the total membership of all affiliated plus non-affiliated organizations represented at the World Congress, showed a decline from 159 million in 1965 to 153 million in 1969.

B. Governing Bodies

226. The present structure of the WFTU dates mainly from the 1969 Congress when in the aftermath of the preceding year's events in Czechoslovakia a number of changes were made.

1. Congress

227. The highest authority of the WFTU continues to be the World Trade Union Congress. It meets about every four years, and all affiliates are entitled to be represented according to their size. That follows the practice in other international trade union organizations. What is different about WFTU congresses is the generously sponsored presence of exceedingly large numbers of observers and representatives from nonaffiliated organizations. The constitutional basis for the presence and active participation of nonaffiliated organizations was laid at the 1969 Congress which decided that 'Organizations which are not members of the WFTU can be associated with its activities . . . and may take part in the discussion of all problems and the adoption of resolutions concerning action with which they have been associated'. In consequence, at the 1978 Congress only 70 of the 124 national centres present were affiliates of the WFTU. Of the total number of organizations represented 104 were members of the WFTU or TUIs and 174 were non-members. It may be assumed that the presence of the many guests and observers is intended to enhance the WFTU's claim to being the most representative labour international and to create the impression that its advocacy of world labour unity is meeting an ever wider response.

2. General Council

228. The General Council ranks just below the World Congress in the hierarchy of governing bodies. It consists of one full and one deputy member from each affiliated national centre, each non-affiliated centre [sic] having a member union affiliated with one of the Trade Union Internationals, and each Trade Union International. At the Ninth Congress in 1978, 66 representatives (and an equal number of deputies) were chosen from the first category, eight from the second, and eleven from the third, thus a total of 85 members and 85 deputy members.

3. Executive Bureau

229. The reorganization of the structure in 1969 merged two previously distinct bodies – the Executive Committee and the Executive Bureau – into a newly constituted Executive Bureau which meets every four months and which may be regarded as an important policy-making body. The Bureau consists of the president (currently Sandor Gaspar of Hungary), the general secretary (currently Enrique Pastorino of Uruguay), three vice presidents, and various other members representing major affiliated organizations. Their actual number is set by each congress. The Ninth Congress set it at 28 full members in addition to the five officers.

4. Secretariat

230. The Secretariat, which does the daily work of the organization, is now composed of a general secretary, a deputy general secretary, and six secretaries. It supervises the several administrative departments, including Press and Information, Education and Training, Relations with National Centres, Trade Union Internationals, Economic and Social Questions, UN and Specialized Agencies, Administration and Finance, and individual sections for the world's major geographic areas.

231. In addition to its regular governing bodies, the WFTU also maintains a number of ad hoc committees and commissions to deal with specific issues, such as young workers, women, multinational companies, and others. In line with the policy of mixed attendance at world congresses the membership of these committees, too, may include representatives of organizations not affiliated with the WFTU.

5. The 1969 Reorganization

232. It would appear that the main effects of the 1969 reorganization were twofold. First, the Executive Bureau was strengthened at the expense of the Secretariat. For example, the Secretariat now cannot on its own initiative make statements in the name of the WFTU as it did before 1969. The size of the staff has apparently been reduced, and it now functions more as an administrative office than a policy making body. The 'restructuring' was undoubtedly due to the determination of the Soviet Union to ensure that the Secretariat would never again embarrass the Soviet Union as it had over the issue of Czechoslovakia in 1968 (see below).

233. The second effect of the reorganization was to make the new Executive Bureau more representative than its predecessor. The previous and numerically much smaller Executive Bureau had been dominated by the Eastern European Communist countries and a few others with strong Communist-led national labour centres. This arrangement had left little room at the top of the WFTU hierarchy for the smaller and weaker Communist labour organizations from other areas. It must, of course, be kept in mind that before 1969 there was also an Executive Committee on which there was ample room for representatives of lesser organizations, but it was of only secondary importance.

C. Finances

234. The financial affairs of the WFTU remain largely inscrutable, although possibly not quite so much nowadays as in the past. For example it is still not known whether the WFTU relies entirely on contributions from its affiliates or receives sizable subsidies from outside sources. (Income from the sale of publications and other miscellaneous revenues cannot be very significant.) In the absence of an independent audit one can not know the true state of affairs. The possibility can certainly not be excluded that a sizable portion of expenses is underwritten by the Soviet Union, over and above the hefty dues paid by the AUCCTU. It is also possible, however, that the WFTU is expected to get along more or less on its income from affiliation fees. Actually, there is some evidence for the second alternative. In 1966, during an acute phase of the Sino-Soviet split, the WFTU accused its Chinese affiliate of being in arrears with its contributions by almost one million dollars. It was evident at the time that the WFTU was experiencing acute financial difficulties, and for a while the official monthly organ, *World Trade Union Movement*, appeared only every other month. The difficulties led the (now defunct) Executive Committee to establish a supplementary fund to which the more solvent affiliates were invited to make contributions in excess of their normal obligations.

235. The Secretariat draws up an annual budget which in the past has always been kept secret but was for the first time made public in sketchy form for the 1976 fiscal year. The total amount of regular contributions anticipated for 1976 was some $1.6 million. Of this sum, about $400,000 (25 per cent) was to be distributed among the Trade Union Internationals (see below) which depend on the WFTU for their income. About 4 per cent of the total was set aside to pay for WFTU meetings, and 6.5 per cent was destined for 'other activities'. Although almost two-thirds of the total budget was thus left unspecified, most of it probably went to pay for salaries and administrative expenses, including scholarships for training and educational programmes, and similar items.

236. If the expenditure budget of $1.6 million was based on an equivalent level of contributions it would indicate a hypothetical affiliation rate equivalent to about $9.00 per thousand of affiliated members. This assumes, however, that the reported membership of 180 million is a fairly accurate figure and assumes further that all affiliated organizations pay their obligations. Of course, these are very unrealistic assumptions. Instead it is more likely either that the actual affiliation fee is well in excess of $9 per thousand members or else that there is a very substantial subsidy from government sources. For comparative purposes the ICFTU's affiliation fee in 1976 was about $60 per thousand members and was scheduled to rise to $80 by 1978.

237. Like the ICFTU, the WFTU maintains an International Solidarity Fund which is apparently kept separate from the regular budget. Information which is unfortunately well out-of-date indicates that this fund was reported to have spent $1.3 million during a forty-month period between 1 January 1962 and 30 June 1965. At this rate annual expenditures would have averaged $325,000. A breakdown of expenditures for the early 1960s indicates that about 60 per cent was spent for activities in underdeveloped countries, and 25 per cent was devoted to what was called 'the national liberation struggle, to the activity of Solidarity Committees and as aid to struggles for trade union rights and to the victims of anti-trade union persecution'. Another 15 per cent was reported to have been used to support strikes and other conflicts in unspecified areas. According to more recent information the Solidarity Fund received nearly one million dollars for 1975. Of this sum 20 per cent (almost $200,000) was spent on 'the struggle against imperialism, colonialism, Fascism and the monopolies'.

238. On the basis of these figures only a very sketchy comparison between the WFTU and the ICFTU can be made. In absolute figures the WFTU appears to have a somewhat smaller income than the ICFTU despite its much larger nominal membership. The total projected income for the WFTU in 1976 was some $2.6 million (made up of $1.6 million for the regular budget and $1.0 million for the Solidarity Fund). By contrast the ICFTU collected in 1974 about $3.0 million (made up of $2.0 million in affiliation fees and $1.0 million in voluntary contributions). However, one should not overlook the fact that the WFTU spends a significant proportion of its administrative expenditures in Czechoslovakia. Costs and living standards there are much lower than in Belgium where the ICFTU has its headquarters. Aside from possible subsidies, the WFTU also benefits financially from services furnished free or below cost by its Eastern European affiliates and their governments.

D. Trade Union Internationals

239. Like other confederal internationals, the WFTU is not well suited to deal with specific industrial issues. It is, after all, composed of national trade union centres whose interests cut across specific industries and occupations and whose concerns – as national centres – are mainly with political issues. Unable to come to terms with the International Trade Secretariats in the protracted negotiations that were carried on between 1945 and 1948, the WFTU was left at the time of the split in 1949 without an organizational apparatus to address issues of concern to unions in specific industries and occupations. To fill the gap it rapidly established a set of so-called International Trade Departments, later called Trade Union Internationals (TUIs). These were intended to be the counterparts of the International Trade Secretariats.

240. Since 1959 there are eleven Trade Union Internationals, each one covering an industrial or occupational sector, as follows:
Forestry and Plantations
Food, Tobacco, Hotel and Allied Industries
Construction, Wood and Building Materials Industries
Oil, Chemical and Allied Industries
Commerce (Offices and Banks)
Teachers
Public and Allied Employees
Metal and Engineering Industries
Miners
Textiles, Clothing, Leather and Fur
Transport, Ports and Fisheries

The individual unions which constitute the TUIs are by and large drawn from the same constituency as that of the WFTU. That means that their national centres are for the most part affiliated with the WFTU.

241. The highest authority of each TUI is its Administrative Committee which usually meets annually. The top official is the general secretary who also serves as chairman of the administrative Committee. Under a 1966 decision of the WFTU General Council, each TUI was instructed to adopt its own constitution. Paradoxically the order was intended to create the appearance of substantial TUI independence from the WFTU and to enable the TUIs to undertake joint actions with other autonomous international bodies. Nevertheless it seems that the TUIs have not played much of an independent role. Unlike the International Trade Secretariats, which almost without exception are financially and organizationally independent from the ICFTU, the TUIs are financially dependent on, and politically directed by, the WFTU. Although they participate at least nominally in the formulation of WFTU policies by virtue of their representation at WFTU congresses, on the General Council, and on the Executive Bureau, they are ultimately expected to adhere to the policies of the WFTU. Just as the WFTU has sought to draw its most prominent officials – president and general secretary – from countries other than Eastern Europe, some TUIs have recruited their general secretaries from unions in non-Communist countries. Nevertheless a large proportion of TUI member unions are concentrated in Communist countries where unions do not engage in independent industrial action.

242. In recent years, the TUIs have sought to establish links with International Trade Secretariats and other national and international trade union bodies. These efforts have been furthered by detente in general and by specific emphasis on the importance of united working class action in coping with the excessive power of multinational corporations. Such appeals, especially when couched in terms of shared industrial interests, have occasionally been successful. In fact, an impressive list of meetings sponsored, organized, convoked or in other ways promoted by the TUIs and by no means limited in attendance to TUI member organizations was presented to the ICFTU Executive Board at its November 1976 meeting as an illustration of Communist efforts to acquire an international trade union legitimacy.

E. Publications

243. During most of its existence, the WFTU has published two periodicals – a monthly magazine and a newsletter. The magazine is the *World Trade Union Movement* (since 1949), which now appears in Russian, English, French, German, Spanish, Rumanian, Swedish, Finnish, Arabic and Japanese. It claims a circulation of 45,000 in some 70 countries and serves as a forum for important policy statements. The WFTU's first newsletter was a weekly *Information Bulletin*, later replaced by a succession of similar publications under various titles. The current WFTU newsletter is called *Flashes from the Trade Unions*, and it is published in English, French, Russian, Arabic and Spanish. The first issue appeared in 1967.

244. In addition to these regular publications, the WFTU also issues special target publications. Starting in 1968, for example, a quarterly publication, *The WFTU and Vietnam* (later renamed *The WFTU and Indochina*), appeared for some time. In 1969 several issues of a *WFTU/AATUF Special Bulletin* were published in three languages – English, French and Russian – to prepare for and publicize an Afro-European Anti-Monopolies Conference. Other bulletins, including *WFTU-Arab Countries, WFTU-Chile,* and *WFTU-Portugal* have been published to tailor WFTU propaganda to specific events and issues. Also, each of the Trade Union Internationals publishes its own monthly bulletin.

245. To list the main themes of WFTU publications would be tantamount to a review of the WFTU's overall aims. The principal stress is on the brilliant and ever rising achievements of the Communist countries, the abject failures and hopeless prospects of the Western countries (the ever deepening but curiously everlasting crisis of capitalism), and the imperative need for world labour unity. Adjusted to particular circumstances, these themes serve to promote most WFTU campaigns and, more or less conspicuously, the prevailing aims of Soviet foreign policy.

246. Special emphasis is allotted to the less developed countries, wherever possible in the context of past colonial exploitation, and there are frequent exposures of the sinister neocolonialist and imperialist designs of the West. Another theme often repeated is the image of the WFTU as an invincible force for working class solidarity, world labour unity, peace, cooperation and harmony among all working people regardless of race, colour, or political beliefs. By contrast, the WFTU's adversaries are held directly or indirectly responsible for whatever divisiveness, conflict, reaction, racism, and other evils beset the world.

II. Aims, Policies, and Activities

A. Avowed Aims

247. As the constitution puts it, the WFTU exists 'to improve the living and working conditions of the people of all lands'. More specifically the constitution proclaims the WFTU's primary aims to be:

a. To organize and unite within its ranks the trade unions of the whole world irrespective of considerations of race, nationality, religion, or political opinion;
b. To assist, whenever necessary, the workers in countries socially or industrially less developed in setting up their trade unions;
c. To carry on the struggle for the extermination of all fascist forms of government and every manifestation of fascism, under whatever form it operates and by whatever name it may be known;
d. To combat war and the causes of war, and to work for a stable and enduring peace.

248. While the avowed aims might be acceptable even to most trade unions not affiliated with the WFTU, the apparent emphasis on organizing and other trade union tasks is in practice subsidiary to a political agenda which serves to promote the foreign policy objectives of the Soviet Union and the countries associated with it. Examples drawn from an earlier period would include the WFTU's expulsion of the Yugoslav unions in 1950 at the height of the Stalin-Tito controversy and the support of Soviet military action in East Germany in 1953 and Hungary and Poland in 1956. More recently, of course, the WFTU was particularly active in mobilizing trade union opinion against U.S. involvement in Vietnam and on behalf of Arab positions in the Middle East. It has often protested nuclear tests by Western powers, though never those conducted by the Soviet Union. During the Cuban missile crisis it attacked the U.S. blockade but made no mention of the presence of Soviet missile sites. Over the years it has denounced the Marshall Plan, the North Atlantic Treaty Organization, the European Economic Community, and virtually all other efforts of Western countries to establish supranational economic, political, and military structures. Solidarity with national liberation movements and against colonialists and neocolonialists is also a frequent subject of WFTU declarations. In this connection, the WFTU has frequently organized 'solidarity days' or 'solidarity weeks' with the workers and people of South Africa, Spain, Korea, the Arab countries, Chile, and others.

249. Over the years the WFTU has made repeated efforts to stage conferences on subjects designed to have wide appeal: young workers, women workers, the environment, social insurance, multinational companies and others. The aim has been to attract maximum support from non-Communist labour groups and to project a more credible trade union image. Yet the task is not an easy one. Domestically, most WFTU affiliates are precluded from expressing serious criticism of the social and labour policies of their own governments and ruling parties. Criticism from the WFTU itself would not be tolerated either. That restriction leads to a clear distinction between the ICFTU and WCL on one hand and the WFTU on the other. While the first two engage in constant and unrelenting criticism of employers in the Western orbit, the WFTU, though eagerly joining all such protests, may express only praise for the conditions prevailing in Communist countries.

250. Criticism thus being out of the question, except if it is directed against the West or selected less developed countries, the WFTU's effort to achieve an appearance of trade union legitimacy has had to concentrate on the image. In that pursuit the WFTU sometime ago modified the preamble of its constitution by acknowledging the importance of trade union independence from political parties and governments. The applicable provision is carefully worded, however, so as to make it quite clear that the new stress on independence is not designed to overturn established relations that already exist between trade unions, governments, and political parties. That limitation constitutes, of course, a vital qualification, for it leaves undisturbed the acknowledged guidance and direction which the ruling Communist parties provide for trade unions and other social institutions in accordance with the constitutions of the various trade union federations in Communist countries.

251. The WFTU has made a considerable effort to build up its position at the UN in general and particularly in the International Labour Organization (ILO) by stressing its commitment to improved international standards of human and trade union rights and its condemnation of the violations of such rights in a wide range of countries other than those under Communist rule. Both at the ILO and away from it, it has regularly led or participated in efforts to mobilize public opinion against governmental measures hostile to trade unionism or directed explicitly against WFTU affiliated organizations, their leaders, and sympathizers. In recent years many of these efforts have concentrated on Chile. Formerly they aimed at Spain, Portugal and Greece.

252. The training programmes sponsored by the WFTU are intended primarily for the less developed countries. Among the major schools operated in conjunction with WFTU affiliates are the International Trade Union College in Moscow, the Georgi Dimitrov Trade Union School in Sofia, Bulgaria, the Fritz Heckert Trade Union College in Bernau, East Germany, and the

Lazaro Peña School in Havana. Regular seminars are also held in Prague at the Czech Trade Union School, while smaller training programmes are offered in cooperation with the WFTU in a number of countries, including Algeria, Guinea, Martinique, Guadeloupe, and Mali. According to the WFTU publication, *Flashes*, over 2,000 trade unionists attended WFTU and affiliated country training schools in 1976.

253. On the issue of the multinational corporations the WFTU has had to cope with a rather awkward situation. As early as 1962 it convened a consultative conference on the subject and then followed up with a conference in 1963 to create a World Trade Union Committee for Consultation and Unity of Action Against the Monopolies. It was also one of the principal participants in the World Trade Union Conference Against Multinational Companies held in Santiago, Chile, in April 1973. However, under conditions of detente the Soviet Union and the other Eastern European countries sought out the technology often available in practice only through cooperative arrangements with multinationals. That seemed to be in contradiction to the anti-multinationals position.

254. To defend itself against attacks of inconsistency the WFTU adopted an interesting stand. In an article in the September 1976 issue of *World Trade Union Movement* it asserted that in essence it was fighting the multinational corporation on two levels. First, it was helping to promote solidarity between workers the world over in their battle against capitalist exploitation by the multinationals. It was doing this by expressing the 'moral support' of workers in Communist countries for workers in capitalist countries. Second, the WFTU claimed that trade between Communist and capitalist countries was strengthening the Communist countries in their historic struggle. Such trade would hasten the day when the workers of the world would be liberated from capitalist exploitation by the complete victory of world communism. The WFTU went on to buttress its position by citing a number of points on behalf of East–West trade. First, trade promotes an international division of labour which results in gains to all trading partners. Second, it provides a basis for world peace. Third, multinationals which build plants in Communist countries must work to the specifications of the Communist countries and therefore cannot exploit Communist workers.

255. Given, then, the general position that economic links between Communist countries and capitalist countries are desirable, dealings by Communist countries with the appropriate economic body in capitalist countries, which happens to be the multinational firm, are unavoidable. It then becomes primarily the responsibility of the workers in capitalist countries to change this situation. This viewpoint was articulately expressed by Georges Séguy, General Secretary of the French CGT, in the March 1975 issue of *World Trade Union Movement*:

'It does not depend upon the socialist states whether multinational companies survive or disappear; that depends mainly on the struggle of the workers in the capitalist countries in alliance with other anti-monopolist sections of society and with the support of international working class solidarity.

256. Accordingly, the WFTU has continued to attack the multinationals, while expressing staunch support for East–West trade and other economic, technical, and scientific relations. The ultimate collapse of capitalism may be inevitable, but in the meantime it does no harm to draw all possible benefits from its achievements.

B. Relations with Member National Centers

257. The WFTU has always tried to project an image of complete internal harmony and unanimity. This is in accordance with the view that the contradictions inherent in capitalist society have been resolved in the Communist countries under the infallible guidance of the ruling Communist parties. Despite the façade of unity, however, the WFTU has had to contend with several internal disputes. These included the Yugoslav–Soviet dispute in 1950, the Sino–Soviet split in 1966, and the Czechoslovak crisis in 1968. In addition there are continuing differences between the labour organizations of the Soviet Union and various countries. Given the closeness of party-union ties in Communist organizations, the disputes reflect the larger differences between the Communist party of the Soviet Union and certain national Communist parties. Conflicting state interests may, of course, also be involved.

258. The first internal dispute after the disaffiliation of the unions from Western democracies in 1949 was the USSR–Yugoslav split. In 1950, the Executive Committee of the WFTU expelled the Yugoslav trade unions. At that time the WFTU organ, *World Trade Union Movement*, condemned the 'Tito clique' for having 'restored capitalism in Yugoslavia' and having transformed it 'into a base for imperialist aggression against the USSR and the People's Democracies.' Several years later, during the Khruschev period, the line changed, and in 1956 the WFTU invited the Yugoslavs to rejoin. The latter did send observers to various WFTU meetings from 1961 on, but they have so far declined to reaffiliate. Evidently Yugoslavia prefers to go its own way in international labour, even if that way sometimes parallels the way of the WFTU.

259. The most serious rift in the WFTU has been between China and the Soviet Union. In the early 1960s, the once seemingly close relationship between the two countries began seriously to deteriorate. Reflecting ever greater tensions between the respective states and ruling parties, the relations between Soviet and Chinese trade union representatives in the WFTU worsened rapidly from 1963 on. Because the appearance of unity was very important to the Soviet side, the initial quarrels with the Chinese were at first kept from surfacing. Before long, however, the Chinese began to attack the WFTU openly as an instrument of Soviet foreign policy and Soviet 'revisionism'.

260. The first open breach occurred at the 13th General Council meeting in Budapest in October 1964. The Chinese and Albanian delegates objected to certain declarations about 'progress in the Socialist countries', meaning progress in the Soviet Union and Eastern Europe, and launched attacks on the Soviet Union. The representatives from North Korea, North Vietnam and Indonesia – all three under Chinese influence – criticized General Secretary Saillant's report for its erroneous emphasis on 'peaceful coexistence'. They advocated more direct attacks on U.S. imperialism because that was at that time the general line of Chinese foreign policy. The Chinese also expressed their intention to refuse to make any further financial contributions to the WFTU until the WFTU 'admits its mistakes self-critically'.

261. To dramatize their discontent with the WFTU's adherence to the policies of the 'capitulationist and revisionist Khruschevite splitters' in the Soviet Union, the Chinese gradually escalated their unconventional expressions of protests by disruptive behaviour at various WFTU and TUI meetings. Several physical confrontations occurred at the 16th session of the General Council in Sofia, Bulgaria, in December 1966. In the end the Chinese and Albanians were expelled from that meeting.

262. Since that time China has not been represented at WFTU meetings, although places are still reserved for Chinese representatives on the Executive Bureau. Albania has also refused to attend WFTU meetings as long as the Chinese are not represented. Technically, then, China and Albania may still be WFTU members. At least they have never formally disaffiliated, nor have they been officially expelled.

263. Shortly after the events in Sofia the All-China Federation of Trade Unions was dissolved in the course of the Cultural Revolution. Recently, enterprise-level and provincial trade union bodies have been reestablished, but a national federation does not yet exist. Nor has China so far resumed relations with international labour bodies, not even at the ILO where since 1972 the People's Republic has held the Governing Body seat till then occupied by the Republic of China (Taiwan).

C. The Reorganized Secretariat

264. The next serious rift in the WFTU occurred over the invasion of Czechoslovakia by five Warsaw Pact countries in August 1968. Because WFTU headquarters were located in Prague, it was virtually impossible for the Secretariat to ignore the event. Louis Saillant, then still General Secretary of the WFTU and generally regarded as a loyal servant of Soviet interests, happened to be on a visit to Hungary when the invasion occurred. He at once informed his hosts that he condemned the occupation. In response to a written request for moral support from the Czech unions, he and Renato Bitossi of Italy, at that time the WFTU president, transmitted a protest letter to the general secretary of the Hungarian Trade Union Council who was himself also a WFTU Executive Committee Member. Saillant asked that the letter be forwarded to the national labour centres of all the countries which had participated in the invasion. (It should be noted that Saillant's and Bitossi's national organizations, the French and Italian Communist parties and trade unions, had also expressed opposition to the invasion.)

265. When the WFTU Secretariat met in Prague for the first time after the invasion it considered Saillant's initial declaration, the Czech unions' appeal for support, and the joint letter of protest by Saillant and Bitossi. By a vote of eight to one, with only the Soviet member of the Secretariat dissenting, it decided to publish the letter which appeared in the French Communist party paper *L'Humanité* on 30 August. The Secretariat also issued a communique which contained the following passage:

'The Secretariat of the WFTU in fully approving this letter expresses its disapproval of the military intervention which contradicts all fundamental principles that form the basis of the life of the WFTU and which are freely established by all the national centers affiliated to the WFTU. The Secretariat expresses its full solidarity to the workers and people of the Czechoslovak Socialist Republic and pays homage to their calm and composure'.

266. Of course, the Soviet Union could not overlook this revolt in an organization from which it had every reason to expect compliance. On 14 September the leaders of the trade unions in Soviet Russia and other Eastern European countries met to condemn 'the attitude of senior officials in the WFTU . . . who disassociated themselves from the intervention of the five countries in Czechoslovakia'. In addition, they discussed the prospects for further 'co-operation' between the trade unions of Czechoslovakia and the other Warsaw Pact states. The next day the union leaders also met with top WFTU officials. Agreement was reached, no doubt only under enormous pressure, to strengthen the WFTU on the basis of the class struggle and proletarian internationalism. In other words, it was decided that the WFTU would fall in line with the policies of the Soviet Union.

267. In the end, Czechoslovakia became 'normalized' under Soviet occupation. Saillant, who had collapsed with a heart attack soon after the invasion, was first temporarily and then permanently replaced as WFTU General Secretary by his deputy, Pierre Gensous, another Frenchman. (Later Saillant was made honorary president of the WFTU. He died in 1974.) The other seven secretaries of the WFTU who had voted to condemn the Soviet invasion were all replaced at the next WFTU Congress in 1969, except for Pierre Gensous who was confirmed as General Secretary. A substantial portion of the staff – perhaps 40 per cent and especially the Czechs among them – were removed. In fact, the entire structure of the WFTU was reorganized to preclude another internal revolt. As already noted above, the Secretariat also lost the right to speak in the name of the WFTU. Technically the issue of the invasion of Czechoslovakia was not on the agenda of the 1969 Congress. That may have been due to an understanding between the Soviet Union and the French, Italian, and other Western European WFTU affiliates according to which the Soviet trade unions would not insist on a retraction of the anti-invasion communique issued by the Secretariat if the Western Europeans forebore to mention the invasion and the occupation in their speeches.

268. The success of the realignment can be measured in part by the WFTU's utter silence during the violent 1976 worker protests in Poland against the prevailing conditions of life and work. The WFTU simply ignored the affair as though it had not taken place.

269. In contrast to the open rifts of the 1960s the Rumanians and the Italians (before their exit in 1978) adopted over the years a more subtle strategy of achieving more autonomy, decentralization, and regionalization. In formulating their position inside the WFTU, the Italian Communist leaders sought not only to reflect the doctrinal and tactical changes in Italian communism but also had to take into account the views of a substantial left-wing socialist minority in the ranks of the CGIL which was usually unenthusiastic about the WFTU situation. Of course the development of cooperation between the three Italian labour centres – CGIL, CISL, and UIL – and certain of their affiliated national unions also contributed to CGIL efforts to pursue an independent course in the WFTU. The Rumanians, while maintaining a rigid Communist dictatorship domestically, regarded their initiatives in the WFTU as part of a more general determination to achieve a maximum of independence in their foreign policy.

270. On certain occasions, the Poles and Hungarians also expressed cautious support for more liberalization in the WFTU, but in such a way as never to let any doubt arise about Poland's basic acceptance of Soviet leadership. Within this context, Sandor Gaspar, the General Secretary of the National Trade Council of Hungary, said at the Eighth WFTU Congress in 1973 that the special position of trade unions in Communist countries had become a subject of misunderstanding because they were too entwined with party and state activities. He admitted that mistakes had probably been made by trade union leaders in failing to convince their people of the importance of trade unions; the unions had chosen the simpler solution and had remained in the shadow of the party.

271. In response to steady pressure from the Italians and the Rumanians, the WFTU agreed in principle in 1966 for the first time to permit more scope for regional activities in those areas 'where there appears to be a community of demands and where specific conditions exist expressing the common interests of the workers' (Article 14 of the WFTU Constitution). Furthermore, the General Council that year agreed to grant national trade union organizations the right to disregard any WFTU decision which was inapplicable to their country. The Eighth Congress in 1973 approved the CGIL's proposal to create an 'associate membership' status, weaker than full membership, in order to retain the Italians as affiliates but allowing them to follow an independent policy. The French CGT opposed the proposal, but that was before the French Communist party itself adopted the position generally referred to as Eurocommunism. The proposal would not have carried, of course, without Soviet support. Subsequently the CGIL shifted to the new associate membership status to enable it to join the European Trade Union Confederation (see below) and also to continue its generally successful policy of close relations with the non-Communist labour organizations in Italy.

272. However, the loosening of the reins turned out in the end to be insufficient to prevent the Italian demand for complete autonomy. After having gradually withdrawn the Italian nationals on the WFTU staff and expressing in ever stronger terms its dissatisfaction with the WFTU as 'an outdated and useless instrument', CGIL severed its ties completely in March 1978. One of the stated reasons was that the decision to hold the Ninth World Trade Union in Prague in April 1978 constituted an unacceptable provocation because of the many instances of recent human rights violations in Czechoslovakia.

273. Although the French CGT did not join the Italians, French criticism of WFTU policies was sharper than ever before and could easily be viewed as preparation for an eventual disaffiliation. The CGT accused the WFTU of still being tied to the spirit of the Cold War, lacking tolerance for diversity, and losing credibility by concentration on the problems of workers in capitalist and Third World countries without ever admitting the existence of such problems in Communist countries. As demonstration of its unhappiness the CGT did not allow its own Pierre Gensous to seek another term as WFTU general secretary, nor did it nominate a replacement. The key position went instead to Enrique Pastorino, a Uruguayan, who had previously served as WFTU president.

D. Relations with Regional Bodies

274. Unlike the ICFTU, the WFTU has usually rejected opportunities to develop regional organizations as an integral part of its structure, although that position may now be changing. Policy direction from a single headquarters was for many decades an uncontested principle of Communist internationalism, as originally formulated by Lenin for the operation of the Comintern and Profintern. Moreover, the Soviet Union had no intention of releasing its overall control of the WFTU by tolerating the establishment of decentralized regional bodies that might acquire in time a measure of authority of their own. It was more efficacious to develop friendly relations with already existing independent regional organizations than to compete with them, especially when there were reasonable prospects for gaining their endorsement of WFTU policies.

275. In Latin America the first regional organization to work with the WFTU had been the CTAL. Actually it predated the WFTU by some ten years and participated in the founding meetings from which the WFTU emerged in

1945. Under the highly personal leadership of Vicente Lombardo Toledano, a Mexican Marxist, CTAL's ideology was always close to that of the WFTU. During the 1950s, however, CTAL went into a steep decline from which it never recovered. It ended its existence in 1964. Its place was later taken by the Standing Congress for Latin American Trade Union Unity (CPUSTAL), nominally an independent body but in fact a close WFTU ally. The WFTU and CPUSTAL have cooperated closely in a number of ventures, including jointly-sponsored regional conferences. Indeed, for all practical purposes CPUSTAL operates as a kind of WFTU regional organization for Latin America.

276. The WFTU has also maintained relations with, and has given financial support to, the International Confederation of Arab Trade Unions (ICATU), an organization formed in 1956 under Egyptian leadership and with strong encouragement from President Gamal Abdel Nasser. Cooperation between the WFTU and the ICATU was institutionalized with the formation of a Joint Working Committee in 1968, but after deterioration of relations between the Soviet Union and Egypt the Joint Committee languished until ICATU removed its seat to Baghdad. It has been meeting about twice a year to coordinate seminars, propaganda, and positions in international bodies on matters of common interest to ICATU and WFTU. Of course the WFTU has invariably endorsed ICATU attacks on Israel and will certainly continue to do so.

277. The relationship between the WFTU and African regional organizations has been somewhat more complicated. The WFTU first cooperated closely with the Pan-African *Union Générale des Travailleurs d'Afrique Noire* (UGTAN) after it was formed in 1957 and even granted it a courtesy seat on the WFTU General Council. Based on Marxist-led Guinea, the UGTAN campaigned actively against French colonialism in Africa, but after the ex-French colonies acquired independence, UGTAN became suspect among the new African governments as a channel for Guinea-inspired pro-Soviet activities. Most UGTAN affiliates outside Guinea were dissolved by the Francophone West African successor states and reconstituted as independent national bodies.

278. The WFTU's African interests shifted to the All-African Trade Union Federation (AATUF) when the latter was founded by the so-called Casablanca bloc under Ghanaian leadership in 1961. AATUF, like most other regional labour groups with which the WFTU has maintained relations, remained nominally nonaligned, but the WFTU extended substantial financial support and sponsored numerous joint AATUF/WFTU conferences and seminars. In 1969 a Joint WFTU/AATUF Working Committee was set up 'to combat imperialist infiltration in Africa and to resist the influence of colonialism and neo-colonialism'. Subsequently, however, AATUF succumbed to a combination of disapproval of its Communist connections and to the pressures of neutralist Pan-African regionalism.

279. A new African regional labour body, the Organization of African Trade Union Unity (OATUU), was formed in 1973 by the member states of the Organization of African Unity (OAU). As in the case of AATUF, the OATUU affiliates were not to have any formal links to other international labour organizations. Most member states of the OAU were keen to exercise effective control over their own national labour organizations. They reasoned, correctly, that such an end would be more easily attained by insulating their trade unions as far as possible from contacts with non-African international organizations. The WFTU's initially hostile attitude to this approach did not last very long. It soon agreed to establish bilateral relations with the OATUU – as did the ICFTU and WCL. Meetings between WFTU and OATUU leaders now occur quite regularly. In fact, the two organizations have on several occasions entered into formal agreements on matters of common interest, including the struggle against apartheid in South Africa, the promotion of a new international economic order, and opposition to the development of multinational companies in Third World Countries.

280. In Asia. the WFTU has found no autonomous regional body with which to establish relations. Before the Sino-Soviet split, a WFTU regional organization for Asia could all too easily have come under Chinese domination, and in that event the Chinese could have turned the regional body against the Soviet Union. However, WFTU affiliates in the area do meet from time to time as a group, most recently in December 1976 in New Delhi in conjunction with a WFTU Executive Bureau meeting. That Executive Bureau meeting adopted a resolution inviting the WFTU's Asian affiliates to work for a united Asian trade union conference. Late in 1978 the WFTU opened a liaison office for Asia in Ho-Chi-Minh City, Vietnam.

III. Relations with Other Organizations

281. As one would expect, the WFTU maintains close relations with other Communist international organizations. Its congresses are regularly attended by observers from the Women's International Democratic Federation, the World Federation of Scientific Workers, the World Federation of Democratic Youth, the World Peace Council and other such bodies.

282. The WFTU holds accredited observer status with various intergovernmental organizations, including the United Nations Economic and Social Council (ECOSOC), the International Labour Organization (ILO), the Food and Agricultural Organization (FAO), the United Nations Educational, Scientific and Cultural Organization (UNESCO), and the Industrial Development Organization (UNIDO). The WFTU also takes an active part in such UN regional organizations as the Economic Commission for Europe (ECE) and the Economic Commission for Asia and the Far East (ECAFE). Its permanent representatives are accredited to the UN and to its specialized agencies in New York, Geneva, Paris and Rome.

283. Exceedingly important are the WFTU's relations with other international trade union bodies, especially the World Confederation of Labour (WCL) and the International Confederation of Free Trade Unions (ICFTU). Top officials of the WFTU and WCL have been holding regular meetings since November 1970. Some of the meetings have had a specific objective, for example the February 1972 session in Dubrovnik, Yugoslavia, to plan a strategy for breaking the ICFTU's hold over most of the worker seats on the ILO Governing Body. The attempt failed. Other WCL–WFTU sessions have served to review current issues of common interest and, where possible, to record agreement on them, as in the case of apartheid, multinational companies, and the ephemeral goal of working class unity. Additionally the WCL was represented at the 1973 and 1978 WFTU congresses by official observers. For the WFTU such relationships are important mainly as proof of its legitimacy, especially since the ICFTU has refused to extend equivalent recognition. For the small WCL they serve a similar purpose.

284. Relations between the WFTU and ICFTU were for a long time marked by fierce competition and hostility. The WFTU incessantly stressed the theme of 'working class unity', while the ICFTU denied the existence of common interests and objectives. In the early 1970s, however, a subtle change occurred whose origins were primarily linked to the detente policies of key Western European governments and the endorsement of detente by many national trade union organizations. The consequences of this change for WFTU–ICFTU relations have been assessed in another section of this volume, but it should be noted here that one significant WFTU initiative has been the convocation of several all-European (i.e. East and West) trade union conferences, the first one having been held in February 1975 in conjunction with the Second European Regional meeting of the ILO. Although neither the WFTU nor the ICFTU was officially represented at that meeting, the general secretaries of the two organizations met privately in the course of the sessions. Pierre Gensous subsequently announced that bilateral WFTU–ICFTU ties had been agreed upon, but that interpretation was at once denied by the ICFTU.

285. In playing on the unity theme, the WFTU follows the strategy described with unvarnished frankness and self-criticism by the leader of its Czech affiliate, Karel Hoffman, on the occasion of the 26th session of the general Council in Paris in October 1975:

'The report (given by WFTU General Secretary Gensous) correctly emphasized that the WFTU Trade Union Internationals (TUIs) and its member centres must continue to put the main emphasis – particularly in the existing situation – on the question of unity and cooperation. We believe that the member centres should help more in this matter and regularly inform the WFTU about their bilateral and multilateral relations with non-member organizations, because the WFTU can use this information in its initiatives toward the ICFTU and the WCL. The same applies also to relations between trade unions and TUI's non-member unions. With the assistance of these bilateral relations of its centres, the WFTU could strive to establish contacts with representatives of non-member organizations in concrete spheres of the trade unions' extensive activity.

To achieve success in establishing contacts with our partners in non-member organizations and particularly in international centres presumes that we know them, and above all know them well. That means to know their programs, their activities, their tactics, actions, changes in orientation, various currents and tendencies of views and so forth. It would be of help in this respect if the WFTU provided still better substantiated and, above all, more rapid information as far as the situation in the ICFTU and WCL is concerned.'

286. One of the Western labour organizations most responsive to WFTU invitations for closer links has been the British Trades Union Congress (TUC). It also happens to be the largest single ICFTU affiliate. At its 1975 annual meeting, for example, it adopted without opposition a resolution 'that the time is ripe for an initiative to be taken to bring the two world trade union centres, i.e. the WFTU and ICFTU, more closely together'. The resolution, which was similar to others adopted in 1971 and 1973, had the support of the TUC central leadership or at least met with no opposition from them. It has since been reaffirmed. To be sure, the ICFTU has not yet done what the TUC has urged it to do, namely to meet officially with the WFTU in a bilateral session. In fact the ICFTU has repeatedly rejected invitations to do so, but the WFTU has in the past been patient about reaching its objectives. It cannot be faulted for assuming that time as well as ongoing changes in what the Soviet Union calls 'the world balance of forces' are working in its favour.

*Countries represented in the WFTU General Council and WFTU Bureau**
(April 1978)

Africa, Near and Middle East

Angola	Madagascar
Arab Republic of Yemen	Mauritius
Benin	Palestine
Congo	People's Dem. Rep. of Yemen
Djibouti	Reunion
Ethiopia	Somalia
Gambia	South Africa
Guinea-Bissau	Sudan
Iran	Syria
Iraq	Upper Volta
Kuwait	Zimbabwe
Lebanon	

*Countries Represented in the WFTU General Council and WFTU Bureau**
(April 1978)

Americas

Argentina	Guiana (Cayenne)
Brazil	Jamaica
Chile	Martinique
Columbia	Nicaragua
Costa Rica	Panama
Cuba	Peru
Ecuador	Salvador
Guadeloupe	St. Lucia
Guatemala	St. Vincent
Guyana	Uruguay
	Venezuela

Australasia

Australia	Mongolia
Bangladesh	Nepal
China	New Caledonia
DPR Korea	Pakistan
Fiji	Papua New Guinea
India	Philippines
Indonesia	Sri Lanka
Japan	Vietnam
Laos	

Europe

Albania	German Democratic Republic
Austria	Hungary
Bulgaria	Poland
Cyprus	Romania
Czechoslovakia	San Marino
Finland	USSR
France	

* Representation may mean either that a national center is affiliated with the WFTU or that an individual union is affiliated with a Trade Union International.

Chapter VI. The World Confederation of Labour

I. Organization and Structure

287. Whereas the ICFTU continues to draw its main strength from Western European unions with a social-democratic heritage and the WFTU has since 1949 relied predominantly on its Communist-led Soviet and other Eastern European affiliates, the World Confederation of Labour has only recently emerged from a transformation during which it shed its once explicitly Christian identity. In its place it has adopted despite some internal opposition a militant secularistic philosophy that contains elements of humanism, socialism, and syndicalism. Concurrently with this profound philosophical change the WCL has also made a major effort to reorient its activities almost exclusively to the needs of its affiliates in less developed countries. But the hard core of its dues-paying membership is still located in a few Western countries: Belgium, the Netherlands, Switzerland, and the Canadian province of Quebec. (France can no longer be included in this list because the CFDT suspended its membership in 1978.)

A. Membership

288. The WCL claimed at the time of its Evian Congress in late 1973 that it had a worldwide membership of about 14,500,000 in 82 affiliated organizations distributed over 78 countries. The distribution of membership by continent, here rounded off, was given as follows:

Membership of the World Confederation of Labor, 1973

Region	Membership
Latin America	5,300,000
Africa	1,300,000
Asia	3,600,000
Europe	4,200,000
North America (Canada)	170,000
Total	14,570,000

Although more recent data are not available, it is likely that the current total would be lower, if only because the French CFDT with about three-quarters of a million members would now have to be deducted from the European contingent.

289. As in the case of other international trade union organizations the figures are of course inflated, and if regular payment of dues is accepted as the proper criterion for membership, which is by no means the case universally, the degree of inflation is very large. It is doubtful, for instance, that the WCL's Latin American regional affiliate, the CLAT, has a dues-paying membership of anywhere close to a million, although this low estimate should not necessarily be taken as an indication of the extent of the CLAT's influence. It must also be pointed out that a considerable proportion of WCL membership in various parts of the world is derived from workers associations and similar bodies rather than unions. To the extent that the members of such associations also belong to unions affiliated with the ICFTU or WFTU they are probably double-counted. Moreover, since 1973 the WCL has lost several affiliates as a result of adverse political developments, as in Chile, Vietnam and all over Africa. All things considered, therefore, a realistic assessment of the WCL's effective membership must result in much less than even half the claimed figure. About four million would appear to be a reasonable guess.

B. Governing Bodies

290. Like other global trade union internationals the WCL has a confederal structure in which the principal affiliated organizations are the national centres. Also integral to the WCL, rather than autonomous as in the case of the ICFTU, are 12 International Trade Federations.

1. Congress

291. The WCL is administered by a hierarchy of governing bodies consisting of a Congress, a Council, a Confederal Board, and an Executive Committee. The Congress is the general assembly of all affiliated organizations. It convenes every four years, and so far all its meetings have been held in Western Europe. As is customary, the affiliates are represented according to their membership, but in common with practice elsewhere the distribution of delegates somewhat favours the smaller organizations. The Congress is the supreme decision-making body of the WCL. Its major tasks are to define the WCL's position on all issues coming before it and to draw up its future programme of action. The Congress is also charged with selecting the members of the Confederal Board and of the Executive Committee and with approving changes in the rules and constitution. Partly because of overrepresentation and partly as a result of deliberate policies, the role of unions from less developed countries has become increasingly dominant at WCL congresses.

2. Council

292. The Council is a smaller version of the Congress. It is composed of members of the Confederal Board and representatives of affiliated organizations. Its major functions are to draw up the annual budget and set the level of dues and special charges. More generally, it also provides detailed directives based on congress resolutions and deals with other important matters that might arise between congresses. Should there be a vacancy in the posts of general secretary or assistant general secretary in the interval between congresses, the Council is empowered to appoint a replacement.

3. Confederal Board

293. The Confederal Board is elected by the Congress and is composed of at least 22 members, including *ex officio* the president, treasurer, general secretary, and assistant general secretaries. The present Board actually consists of 28 members. In addition there are alternate members for all except the executive officials. At least eight seats on the Board are reserved for the national centres, six for the International Trade Federations, and one each for the WCL regional organizations. Meeting twice a year, the Board exercises general leadership in the WCL and supervises the activities of the Executive Committee. Its explicit duties include setting the time, place, and agenda of the Council meetings and preparing the sessions of the Congress.

4. Executive Committee

294. The Executive Committee at present consists of seven members: the president, treasurer, general secretary, and four assistant general secretaries selected to ensure regional representation. Nominally it is in collective charge of the day-to-day affairs of the WCL, but in practice the administrative work is under the direction of the general secretary, Jan Kulakowski, who holds the highest full-time position. The seat of the organization is in Brussels, Belgium.

C. Finances

295. Because the WCL unfortunately does not publish financial reports, its income and expenditure budgets are not subject to external scrutiny. However, when the 1975 Council meeting adopted a resolution recommending a 12 per cent increase in dues for 1976, the WCL noted in its own publication, *Labor*, that the result would be to raise the level of obligatory affiliation fees to be paid by affiliated national centres to 5.8 Belgian Francs (about $0.12) per member per year, to which one should add another 2.6 Belgian Francs (about $0.04) per member per year from the International Trade Federations.

296. It may be quite safely assumed that this resolution was subsequently endorsed by the affiliated organizations, but it would be hazardous to conclude that the income of the WCL can now be computed by a simple multiplication. Most WCL affiliates are in no financial position to contribute at the official rate, nor are they expected to do so. It would be more prudent to assume that the overwhelming proportion of WCL dues income is derived from the solvent affiliates in Western Europe (especially Belgium and the Netherlands) and perhaps also from Canada. Estimating the total dues-paying membership in Western Europe and Canada to be about two million (1,000,000 for Belgium, 600,000 for the Netherlands, 170,000 for Canada and the remainder for Switzerland and a few other countries) – and more or less discounting the International Trade Federations as a significant source of dues payments – one would guess that total income flowing into the general fund from affiliation fees amounts to perhaps $300,000 per year or even a bit less.

297. There is, however, another source of income that could well be more important. Since 1958, the WCL has maintained besides its general fund an International Solidarity Fund based on more or less voluntary contributions. Affiliates that are financially in a solvent position have been expected to contribute a minimum of one Belgian Franc ($0.02) per member per year into this fund which is intended, as in the case of the ICFTU, to support the special work in less developed countries. The 1968 Congress proceedings revealed, however, that several European affiliates had been making voluntary contributions well in excess of the minimum. Notably the Belgian CSC was reported to have contributed an average of 12 Belgian Francs ($0.25) per member per year. Perhaps in line with this performance and in view also of continued inflation, the expected minimum payment to the ISF has recently been raised to 12 Belgian Francs ($0.25 at current exchange rates) per member per month. That increase could result in a very considerable amount of income, but only if a sufficient number of organizations comply. The Canadian affiliate of the WCL mentioned in its 1972 Convention report that its contribution to the WCL International Solidarity Fund for 1973 would amount to around $56,000, and more recently the Belgian affiliate claimed that it had earmarked about $300,000 for international solidarity purposes in 1974, although it was unclear whether the entire sum, or only part of it, ended up in the WCL's fund. Indirect but important government contributions must also be included here. For example, a sizable portion of the overseas development funds which the Dutch government channels through the Dutch trade unions is remitted to the WCL through its two Dutch affiliates – currently at least $700,000 per year. In any case, the International Solidarity Fund is likely to be a substantial resource, all the more so if its income is supplemented by contributions from affluent organizations which, though not trade unions themselves, believe in the importance of the WCL's work in less developed countries, as for example Catholic charitable groups in West Germany.

298. Unlike the ICFTU, the WCL has not used its Solidarity Fund as an emergency resource for the operation of the secretariat or as a reserve fund to be drawn upon if regular income falls short of operating needs. On the other hand, it does use a certain portion of ISF income to reimburse the secretariat for administrative expenses.

D. Regional Organizations

299. The WCL currently has two official regional organizations, two others having been dissolved in 1974. By far the most important of those remaining is the Confederation of Latin American Workers (CLAT). It was originally founded in 1954 as the Confederación Latinoamericana de Syndicalistas Cristianos (CLASC) by Christian trade unionists from various Latin American countries, and as its name indicates it was conceived more as an organization of trade unionists than of trade unions. It changed its name to Central Latino Americana de Trabajadores (CLAT) in 1971, but it still contains both individual members and organizational affiliates.

1. CLAT

300. Almost from the very beginning, CLASC/CLAT became a rival to the ICFTU's regional affiliate, ORIT. CLAT's leadership regarded ORIT as being under the domination of the North American AFL-CIO and considered its support of business unionism inappropriate to Latin American conditions. Strongly distrusting the intentions of the AFL-CIO, CLAT also rejected ORIT's belief in hemispheric trade union solidarity and emphasized the importance of creating and relying on a purely Latin American organization.

301. Underlying the desired exclusion of North American influences is CLAT's view of the future of Latin America. The central problem facing Latin American workers, according to CLAT, is externally imposed underdevelopment, and the major impediment to its solution is the feudal socio-economic structure and the power and influence of foreign, especially North American, multinationals. Without a revolutionary transformation of Latin American society, the basic needs and aspirations of workers cannot be satisfied. CLAT, therefore, not only rejects as insufficient the concentration of business unionism on immediate demands, but is also convinced that as long as there is a North American presence in the hemispheric trade union ranks the necessary revolutionary transformation cannot be accomplished.

302. In aiming for a social revolution, CLAT has expressed a willingness to work with other organizations that seek to create a socialist and independent Latin America, but in its view trade unions rather than political parties must play the leading role in the coming transformation, for they alone are properly equipped to promote mass participation. Such neo-syndicalist views are fully consonant with CLAT's image of a future society based on worker self-management at every level. In line with the traditions of syndicalism in France and elsewhere, CLAT thus sees the trade union as more than a simple economic organization. Its emphasis on the trade union as the basis for the future community of workers means that priority must be given to the educational and cultural uplifting of workers. Consequently CLAT has operated several international and national study institutes in Venezuela, Costa Rica, Argentina and other countries. Its most ambitious educational venture is a workers' university (UTAL), founded in 1974, whose responsibilities also include research projects.

303. To finance its programme, including the workers' university, CLAT receives support from the WCL International Solidarity Fund, various sympathetic sources in Germany, such as the Konrad Adenauer Foundation, International Solidarity, and the 'German Bishop's Fund', as well as from other European countries. In 1977 it claimed 34 national affiliates (although several were in exile or underground). Estimates of its 'true' strength vary, but according to one informed view it had probably somewhat over a million adherents (not necessarily all dues paying) of whom 60 per cent were peasants and agricultural labourers. Only in Ecuador and the Dominican Republic is a CLAT affiliate a leading trade union centre.

304. The transformation of CLASC/CLAT from a relatively docile Christian association of trade unionists to a militantly secular and syndicalist organization is not unique. Indeed it has been reflected in the programme of the WCL itself. But because of the stridency of CLAT's foremost leader, Emilio Maspero, the regional organization in Latin America has appeared to be more extreme than the parent organization, and there have even been occasions when Brussels headquarters seemed to be incapable of exercising any control over CLAT. However, it would be a mistake to regard the basic relationship between the world centre and the Latin American periphery as hostile. To be sure, some WCL affiliates such as the Protestant CNV in the Netherlands disavow CLAT's extreme revolutionary rhetoric, but such disagreements have usually been subordinated to a valiant search for the widest possible area of agreement.

2. BATU

305. The WCL's Asian regional organization, the Brotherhood of Asian Trade Unionists (BATU), was the last one to be formed. It was founded in 1963 and has its headquarters in the Philippines. At its 1978 (Ninth) Congress, BATU claimed affiliated organizations in Bangladesh, Indonesia, Malaysia, Pakistan, the Philippines, Sri Lanka, and Thailand. It also has liaison groups in India, Singapore, Taiwan, Hong Kong, and Japan. Even if the political situation in Asian countries were more hospitable to WCL organizing efforts, it would still be difficult for an organization with deep Christian antecedents to gain a wide following in a continent where the major religious groups are neither Catholic nor Protestant. As it is, the WCL's claim of 3.6 million Asian members as of 1973 seems to have been extremely optimistic even for that period and would certainly be far from the contemporary reality.

3. PAWC/FOPADESC

306. The Pan-African Workers Congress (PAWC) no longer exists. It was originally organized as the Union Pan-Africaine des Travailleurs Croyants in the former Belgian and French colonies of Africa and renamed PAWC in 1959 with the affiliation of several unions from former British colonies. In 1973 the WCL claimed a total African membership of about 1,300,000, but by then the PAWC's member unions were already experiencing considerable difficulty in maintaining their autonomy and even their very existence. Most African governments had decided to bring the labour movements under close control by creating a unitary national trade union organization into which existing unions were to be compelled to merge. Unable to resist the anti-pluralistic pressures, the PAWC dissolved itself in 1974, and its member unions joined the Organization of African Trade Union Unity. With government tolerance a few affiliates have been able to maintain a direct (dual) affiliation with the WCL. For the purpose of keeping at least a tenuous link among its former African contingents the WCL relies nowadays on FOPADESC, the Pan-African Foundation for Economic, Social, and Cultural Development, whose headquarters are in Lomé, Togo's capital. It is a kind of covert regional WCL body.

4. EO

307. The European Organization (EO), formed in 1958, was dissolved in 1974 so that its affiliates could join a unified European regional organization made up of national centres affiliated both with ICFTU and WCL. This decision was of course not determined by government pressure, but by the voluntary action of the European affiliates of the ICFTU and WCL. The organizations formerly affiliated to the EO have independently continued their affiliation with the WCL. In fact, they constitute its backbone.

E. International Trade Federations

308. The WCL currently has 12 affiliated International Trade Federations claiming a total of over 8,500,000 members. These are specialized industrial bodies composed of individual national unions in agriculture, food production, white-collar employment, wood and construction, energy and related industries, metallurgy, mining, and public service employment. Only two of the International Trade Federations claim over a million members, the International Federation of Trade Unions of Employees in Public Service and the

World Federation of Agricultural Workers, but their figures are not reliable. The officials of almost all ITSs are Belgian or Dutch.

309. Administratively the federations are an integral part of the WCL rather than autonomous bodies. Their tasks are identical with those of the International Trade Secretariats, namely to provide their member unions with services and information that will help them do a more effective job of representing the interests of their members in dealings with employers and governments. But in order to be effective, some minimum size and resource base are required, and most of the International Trade Federations have failed to reach that minimum. Having thus very little significance even for unions in WCL-affiliated national centres, they have lost several member unions to the International Trade Secretariats and have recently suffered further depletion because the French CFDT decided to suspend its affiliation with the WCL. At the 1977 WCL Congress a decision was taken to review the status of the federations, but it is difficult to see how such a review could bring about a significant improvement.

II. Aims and Policies

310. The Christian International, CISC to use its original initials, was founded largely to combat the influence of socialism among Catholic (and to a lesser extent Protestant) workers. To be sure, the Church in its encyclicals also criticized capitalism, but as an alternative to socialist 'materialism' the Church contemplated a corporative and cooperative relationship between capital and labour in which workers would be enabled to play a more active role in the direction of work through their organizations.

311. At the Congress of Liège in 1964 the CISC adopted a new Declaration of Principles which called for rational economic planning to satisfy human needs, a greater role for workers' organizations in economic decision making, a right to work for all, a right to fair working conditions, and cooperation between labour and management on an international scale to solve the world-wide problems of economic development. The declaration considered private ownership as 'essential to the liberty of the individual' but acknowledged that in certain situations nationalization would be necessary and acceptable.

312. Four years later the Luxemburg Congress promulgated a new Declaration of Principles that went considerably further. It was this Congress which changed the name of the Christian International to the World Confederation of Labour. The new conception condemned both capitalism and Marxist state socialism as incompatible with the achievement of a humane economic and social system. Beyond democratic planning it strongly emphasized the non-material needs of workers and insisted that only through the complete integration of the worker into the decision-making process at every level of economic decision making could these needs be fulfilled. In this reformulation, two major ideas were carried over from the CISC to the WCL. One was the insistence that a trade union had to be more than merely an organization for winning economic benefits for workers, and the other held that the trade union movement had to be independent of political parties and governments (and now the Church as well).

313. On this new basis the WCL has tried to present itself as a plausible trade union alternative to its two large competitors – the ICFTU and the WFTU. Against the former it emphasizes its commitment to a revolutionary social transformation and its disdain for mere 'economism'. Against the latter it proclaims its independence from state and party controls. And against both it cites its freedom from involvement in Great Power politics. Its revolutionary programme is designed to be both anti-capitalist and anti-communist. But the main adversary (also referred to in a WCL document as 'the main and most important enemy of the working classes throughout the world') is 'international capitalism with its "spearhead", the multinationals'.

314. Ultimately the WCL envisages the establishment of an egalitarian society based on 'real democracy' and 'true socialism'. What 'real democracy' means is not clear, but whatever it may be it must extend to all political, economic, social, and cultural areas. 'True socialism' probably includes the socialization of the means of production, democratic (rather than imperative or administrative planning), and the eventual disappearance of wage labour through the active participation of workers at every level of decision making.

315. In keeping with its claim to be a genuinely international organization, the WCL has paid considerable attention to the problems of underdevelopment and to the role of trade unions in developing nations. Indeed the weakness of the WCL in the context of industrialized countries has promoted an idealization of the Third World and its trade unions to the point of subordinating virtually all WCL activities to the claimed needs of workers in the less developed countries. In line with this conception the WCL emphasizes the importance of international trade union solidarity and the responsibility of trade unions in the developed nations to come to the assistance of trade unionists in the Third World. Not only does the WCL feel that such solidarity would benefit workers worldwide, but it also accepts the notion that workers in the developed countries have a debt to repay for past exploitation of the Third World through which the workers in the developed nations gained their higher standard of living. The most pernicious obstacles to an indispensable redress of past injustices are imperialism (American and Soviet) and neocolonialism. According to the *Orientation Report* presented as a proposed policy document to the 19th Congress of the WCL in October 1977 – and accepted by that body – neocolonialism has even infiltrated the trade union movement, as 'seen in its most brutal form in the activities of the AFL–CIO in Latin America, Asia and Africa'.

316. Obviously, the WCL has undergone a great transformation since World

War II. However, its present position does contain elements of continuity with its past. The position on workers control, the emphasis on the non-material needs of workers, and the insistence on trade union autonomy can be traced back to earlier Christian principles in support of the idea that workers should play an active and not merely a passive role in determining how they live and work. The WCL also continues to oppose what it calls Marxist materialism, but it has accepted so much of Marx's thought that what it opposes seems to be more the dogmatic and deterministic application of Marx's teachings than Marxism itself.

317. For example, the *Orientation Report* includes a passage on the class struggle ('the hardest lump to swallow for some of our colleagues') which in its perspective and terminology aptly conveys the mainstream of opinion in the WCL:

'The class struggle is an expression of a state of alienation and a way of resolving the problem, a SITUATION imposed by capitalist society and an INITIATIVE by the workers to regain their freedom, their responsibility and their dignity, projecting themselves as a historical force in the construction of a new society.

It must be repeated that history has shown that the privileged classes and the oppressors never WILLINGLY relinquish their position of strength; they have always had to be DEFEATED. Hence the need for the struggle as a WAY (method) of breaking their strong and stubborn resistance, which only gives way when it is beaten, and which must be soundly beaten to open the gates to the complete liberation of the workers.'

Equally revealing of WCL sentiments is another passage from the same section of the *Orientation Report* which holds that:

'It is essential to develop certain situations in greater depth, not through cold intellect, but through the heart and the passions, which makes accepted and understood situations which simple logic is incapable of understanding and accepting. It must therefore be stated quite positively that the central motivation behind this option and the commitment to the class struggle is the love of man, of all mankind, of all men, of justice, freedom and real peace.'

318. Consistent with its general views the WCL does not believe that the present economic difficulties in the world are merely a cyclical occurrence, but rather that they represent a structural crisis in capitalism – a time when the working class everywhere, but especially in the industrialized nations, is faced with growing unemployment and a falling standard of living. The appropriate response according to the WCL is permanent confrontation. Specifically, it calls for opposition to all austerity measures, such as cuts in public expenditures, incomes policies, or retrenchments in social security. But it also views the economic crisis as an opportunity for workers to extend their power and influence, especially through increased worker control at the workplace. Workers should therefore exert pressure on governments to institute reforms that would increase workers' power in the firm and at levels of economic decision-making above the individual firm.

III. Relations with Other Organizations

319. Although – or perhaps because – the WCL is by far the smallest of the international trade union confederations, it has steadily sought to maintain its independence and separate identity, resisting all suggestions from outside and inside that it merge with the ICFTU. Instead it has tried especially since its secularization in 1968 to present itself as a plausible alternative to its two larger rivals. A serious obstacle to this effort has been its small size and its modest growth potential. Size is related in rough proportion to an organization's weight and its capacity for influence. Clearly these have been exceedingly limited, and the WCL has been very sensitive to such considerations, as shown for example by the fact that its membership claims are relatively even more exaggerated than those of the ICFTU and WFTU. The prospects for expansion in Europe are minimal. In fact, there is a reasonable possibility that in the near future the Dutch Catholic federation NKV may follow the French CFDT and disaffiliate. Since January 1976 the NKV and the Dutch socialist trade union federation, NVV, have joined together in a superfederation which still allows a measure of independence for each partner but which is nevertheless moving toward complete fusion. The dynamics of the NVV–NKV relationship, in which the ICFTU-affiliated NVV is by far the stronger partner, have compelled the NKV to advocate with some urgency the resumption of merger negotiations between WCL and ICFTU, but a formal proposal to this effect was rejected by the 1977 WCL Congress. Since that time the NKV has announced its firm intention to leave if the WCL fails to begin merger discussions with the ICFTU before the end of 1978.

320. Resistance to merger talks is strongest among the WCL's affiliates in the less developed countries, particularly in Latin America, but apparently these groups fail, or do not wish, to realize the disastrous implications of the shrinking central base for the standing and influence of the WCL. There are also strong objections to a merger among the top officials of the WCL Secretariat.

321. Outside of Europe, the WCL, like the other internationals, has seen in the developing countries with their vast numbers of unorganized workers an area for potential growth, but in recent years it has had to face increasingly the currently insoluble problem of authoritarian and nationalistic governments hostile to independent unions. Thus the African regional organization, the PAWC, has had to disband; the Asian regional affiliate, BATU, has lost its largest union, the Vietnamese; and CLAT in Latin America, the most militant regional organization, has been hard-pressed by the wave of military regimes that have swept Latin America. Nevertheless, the WCL has indicated its willingness to accept at least some of these developments as 'realities'. According to the WCL, the Organization of African Trade Union Unity (OATUU), on which the African governments have bestowed a monopoly of regional representation, 'expresses the trade union realities on the continent of Africa'.

As regards the International Confederation of Arab Trade Unions (ICATU), the WCL's view has been summarized by the observation that:
'the ICATU is a very politicized trade union structure, because the Arab world considers itself to be at war (cf. the European trade union movement during the second world war), but it embodies trade union realities of the Arab world and forms part of the Third World trade union movement'.

Both OATUU and ICATU are regarded by the WCL as 'privileged partners in [the] renovation' of the international trade union structure, a status that is also extended to the European Trade Union Confederation.

322. Relations with the ICFTU have already been dealt with in the chapter on the ICFTU. Clearly they have had many ups and downs. The WCL has often complained that the larger organization has treated it with 'indifference and disdain' and has at times criticized the ICFTU for 'its unbearable pretension to possessing a monopoly of free and democratic trade union representation'. In Latin America, the WCL admitted in 1968 to the existence of a 'positive state of war' between its own and the ICFTU's regional organization (ORIT). However, with much closer contacts now between national affiliates at European level, the two internationals, especially the WCL, have been under some internal pressure to cooperate more extensively.

323. In fact, inside the WCL the question of restructuring the international labour movement and the role to be played by the WCL in this process has been one of the major topics of discussion since the Evian Congress of 1973. The current official position is that all possible cooperation short of merger with the ICFTU would be appropriate. For some WCL affiliates, however, this does not go far enough. At the 1977 Congress, for example, the Dutch Catholic Federation, NKV, abstained on the vote to approve the most important resolution on the agenda because the section on relations with the ICFTU was expressed in terms which it considered too reticent. Before its departure, the French CFDT was one of the most vocal proponents of the need for a complete reevaluation of the WCL's role in the international labour movement and repeatedly called for more unity of action with other organizations, including unaffiliated unions in Yugoslavia and elsewhere throughout the world. On the other hand, there is at least one WCL affiliate, the Dutch Protestant CNV, which regards the WCL's move to the left as a grave error, so grave that the CNV's continued affiliation cannot be taken for granted anymore.

324. The WCL and the WFTU have maintained formal relations since 1970 through regular meetings for exchanges of views. However, the WFTU has noted with disappointment the preferred position that the WCL accords to the ICFTU. For example, although the WCL and the ICFTU have on several occasions issued joint statements and engaged in joint endeavours on subjects such as Spain, Chile, apartheid, and multinationals, the WCL has refrained from similar common action with the WFTU. The WFTU complains that the WCL has restricted itself to vague agreements for 'concerted' undertakings, but has in practice refused to commit itself to any WFTU proposal. Nevertheless the two organizations exchanged representatives to their congresses for the first time in 1973 and have done so since then. Representatives from CLAT were also present at the 1978 WFTU Congress. In the foreseeable future one should assume that the WCL will want to continue its contacts with the WFTU, if only because both sides benefit from this reinforcement of their status and legitimation.

325. At one time or another, most international trade union organizations have faced the task of defining their identity and justifying their existence to themselves, their constituents, and perhaps even the world at large. None, however, has ever been as introspective as the WCL, nor struggled so much with its conscience. Certainly there is no other international labour movement that is engaged in an almost permanent 'agonizing reappraisal' of its *raison d'être*. Indeed, ever since its conversion from the original Christian social doctrine to a class struggle ideology, the WCL has wrestled, almost Hamlet-like, with the most profound questions of existence. A recent version of its quest was aptly summarized in the 1977 *Orientation Report*:

'The WCL is always searching for its identity. But this is not really a weakness; it is proof rather of its vitality and desire for authenticity. Those who spare themselves the effort of such a search are perhaps afraid that they will find nothing there at the end of the road . . . But when it comes to effective everyday action, this search, this self-questioning is sometimes a heavy cross to bear.

As we have already said, too many questions remain unanswered within the WCL, especially in Europe, because some people have failed to grasp the guidelines laid down. Are we ex-Christians, as they like to call us ironically within the ICFTU? Are we humanist-socialists, as opposed to social democrats or Marxist socialists? Do we really want self-managing socialism, do we know what it is and how to achieve it? In the final analysis, are we for or against the class struggle?'

The sincerity of these sentiments is beyond question. But such preoccupations do appear difficult to reconcile with the more prosaic tasks that international trade unions are expected to accomplish on behalf of their constituent organizations.

World Confederation of Labor (WCL)
*List of Affiliated Organizations**

Country	Organization
Algeria	Union Générale des Travailleurs Algeriéns (UGTA)
Angola	Union Nationale des Travailleurs Angolais (UNTA)
Austria	Fraktion Christlicher Gewerkschaftler im ÖGB
Bangladesh	Bangladesh Sanjukta Sramic Federation

* The African organizations are not affiliated but instead maintain collaborative relations with the WCL.

Country	Organization
Belgium	Confédération des Syndicats Chrétiens de Belgique (CSC/ACV)
Belize	National Federation of Workers (NFW)
Benin	Union Nationale des Syndicats des Travailleurs du Benin (UNSTB)
Botswana	Trade Union Education Centre
Cameroon	Union Nationale des Travailleurs du Cameroun
Canada	Confederation of National Trade Unions (CNTU)
Cape Verde	Sindicatos Caboverdeanos
Central African Empire	Union Générale des Travailleurs du Centraficaine (UGTC)
Chad	Union Nationale des Travailleurs du Tchad (UNATRAT)
Colombia	Confederación General del Trabajo (CGT)
Congo-Brazzaville	Confédération Syndicale Congolaise (CSC)
Costa Rica	Central de Trabajadores Costarricenses (CTC)
Cuba	Solidaridad Trabajadores Cubanos (STC) (in exile)
Cyprus	Democratic Labour Federation of Cyprus (DEOK)
Dominican Republic	Confederación Autónoma de Sindicatos Cristianos (CASC)
	Dominica Amalgamated Workers' Union (DAWU)
Ecuador	Central Ecuatoriana de Organizaciones Clasistas (CEDOC)
El Salvador	Central de Trabajadores Salvadorenos (CTS)
French Guyana	Centrale des Travailleurs Chrétiens de la Guyane (CGTC)
Gabon	Fédération Syndicale Gabonnaise (RESYGA)
Gambia	Gambia Trade Union Congress (GTUC)
Ghana	Trade Union Congress (TUC)
Grenada	Progressive Labour and General Workers' Union (PLGWU)
Guadeloupe	Centrale Syndicale Démocratique de Guadaloupe (CSDG)
Guatemala	Central Nacional de Trabajadores (CTN)
Guinea Bissau	Union Générale des Travailleurs de la Guinée-Bissau (UNTG)
Guyana	Guyana Federation of Trade Unions and Farmers Organizations
Haiti	Fédération Haitienne des Syndicats Chrétiens (FHSC)
Honduras	Central General de Trabajadores (CGT)
India	National Front of Indian Trade Unions (NFITU)

Country	Organization
Indonesia	Federasi Buruh Seluruh Indonesia
	Indonesian Federation of Christian Workers' Associations (KESPEKRI)
	Konsentrasi Golongan Karya Buruh (KONGKARBU-SOKSI)
	Sentral Organizasi Buruh Pantjasila (SOB Pantjasila)
Italy	Associazione Cristiane Laboratori Italiana (ACLI)
Ivory Coast	Union Générale des Travailleurs de la Côte d'Ivoire (UGTCI)
Jamaica	Independent Trade Union Action Council (ITAC)
Kenya	Central Organization of Trade Unions of Kenya (COTUK)
Lesotho	Lesotho Council of Labour (LCL)
Liberia	Liberian Confederation of Labour (LCL)
Lichtenstein	Liechtensteiner Arbeitnehmerverband (LAV)
Luxemburg	Luxemburger Christlicher Gewerkschaftsbund (LCGB)
Madagascar	Cartel National des Organizations Syndicales Malagasy (CARNOSYNA)
	Union des Syndicats Autonomes de Madagascar (USAM)
Malaysia	Malaysan Workers Movement
Mali	Union Nationale des Travailleurs du Mali (UNTM)
Malta	Confederation of Malta Trade Unions (UNTM)
Martinique	Centrale Syndicale Démocratique de la Matinique (CSDM)
Mauritius	Mauritius Labour Congress
	Confédération Nationale du Travail
	Confédération Mauricienne des Travailleurs
Mexico	Frente Auténtico del Trabajo (FAT)
Montserrat	Montserrat Allied Workers Union (MWU)
Netherlands	Nederlands Katholiek Vakverbond (NKV)
	Christelijk Nationaal Vakverbond (CNV)
Netherlands Antilles	Antilliaans Verbond van de Arbeid (AVA)
Nicaragua	Central de Trabajadores Nicaraguenses (CTN)
Niger	Union Nationale des Travailleurs du Niger (UNTN)
Nigeria	Nigerian Labour Congress (NLC)
Panama	Central Istmeña de Trabajadores (CIT)
Paraguay	Federación de Trabajadores Urbanos (FTU)
Peru	Confederación Nacional de Trabajadores (CNT)
Philippines	Federation of Free Workers (FFW)

Country	Organization
Puerto Rico	Frente Unido de Trabajadores Puertorriqueños (FUTPR)
Ruanda	Syndicat Interprofessionel des Travailleurs du Rwanda (SITR)
Santa Lucia	National Workers Union (NWU)
Senegal	Confédération Nationale des Travailleurs du Sénégal
Seychelles Islands	Seychelles Trade Union Congress
	Seychellois Christian Workers Union
Sierra Leone	Sierra Leone Council of Labour (SLCL)
Spain	Solidaridad de Trabajadores Vascos (STV)
	Solidaridad de Obreros de Catalynya (SOC)
Sri Lanka	National Workers Congress (NWC)
St. Vincent	St. Vincent Workers Union
Surinam	Progressieve Werknemers Organisatie (PWO)
Switzerland	Christlich-Nationaler Gewerkschaftsbund der Schweiz (CNG)
	Schweizerischer Verband Evangelischer Arbeiter und Angestellter (SVEA)
Tanzania	National Union of Tanganyika Workers (NUTA)
Thailand	National Council of Thai Labour (NCTL)
Togo	Confédération Nationale des Travailleurs du Togo (CNTT)
Upper Volta	Confédération Nationale des Travailleurs Voltaiques (CNTV)
	Confédération des Syndicats Voltaiques (CSV)
Venezuela	Movimiénto Nacional de Trabajadores para la Liberación (MONTRAL)
	Confederacion de Sindicatos Autonomos de Venezuela (CODESA)

Chapter VII. Independent Regional Federations and Similar Bodies

326. The three international trade union federations reviewed in the preceding chapters – ICFTU, WFTU, and WCL – all claim a global constituency. That means that they gather affiliates from every corner of the world without geographical restrictions. Insofar as they also maintain their own regional organizations, as in the case of the ICFTU and WCL, these are in constitutional form subsidiary bodies whose policies are supposed to conform to the basic principles of the parent organization. (The WFTU's regional organization for Latin America, CPUSTAL, may be nominally independent, but in fact also operates much like a subsidiary body.)

327. Standing apart from this structure is a small group of genuinely independent organizations whose membership is defined by geographical or functional criteria. Historically, independent regional organizations have existed particularly in the Americas and more recently also in Africa, but currently there exist only three such organizations – the European Trade Union Confederation (ETUC), the Organization for African Trade Union Unity (OATUU), and the International Confederation of Arab Trade Unions (ICATU). The last two overlap somewhat in their membership.

328. Not strictly an independent regional organization, but functioning very much as though it were, is the Trade Union Advisory Committee to the Organization for Economic Cooperation and Development (TUAC–OECD). It is technically not a regional body for the simple reason, specified in more detail below, that the intergovernmental agency to which it is attached, the OECD, is itself not limited to countries in a particular region. Instead it defines its constituency primarily in terms of an advanced level of economic development and adherence to a shared set of political-ideological values.

I. Independent Regional Federations

329. No single reason can explain the impetus for the formation of an independent regional federation of trade unions. Some have been established as instruments to further the expansionist or hegemonic ambitions of a particular country or an individual ruler. For example the now defunct Agrupación de Trabajadores Latino Americanos Sindicalistas (ATLAS) was formed under the aegis of Argentine president Juan Perón during his first period in office as a way of rallying the working classes of other Latin American countries behind

Argentine leadership under the doctrine of *Justicialismo*. In similar fashion the All African Trade Union Federation (AATUF) became the regional trade union organ of the so-called Casablanca group of African states and particularly of Ghanaian president Kwame Nkrumah at a time of vigorous competition (the early 1960s) over the ideological direction of the new states on the African continent.

330. Other regional federations have resulted from the attempts of national rulers to insulate the trade unions of a particular region from ideas and influences that run counter to the philosophy of the regionally dominant governments or political organizations. The OATUU, for instance, owes its existence largely to a concerted effort of many African governments to prevent the spread of independent trade unionism in Africa and to legitimate on a region-wide basis the subordination of labour organizations to their national governments.

331. Yet another reason is linked to the integration of states in a particular region. To illustrate, the adoption of the Schuman Plan for the European coal and steel industries and subsequently the establishment of the European Economic Community led the trade unions in the participating countries to set up regional structures of their own as vehicles to express their views and interests in matters of special concern to them, notably in social and labour policies.

332. The following presentation of regional trade union federations is organized by geographical subdivisions according to the major regions of the world. It will review not only the presently existing bodies but will also cover their predecessors.

A. Europe

333. For Europe, regionalism as an operating concept became a reality only after the Second World War. Before 1945 no intergovernmental bodies existed that might have stimulated the emergence of a regional trade union grouping. Besides, the principal international trade union federation in the prewar period, the IFTU, was composed mostly of European members, and insofar as issues arose that were of eminent concern to European labour as a whole, the IFTU was deemed to be an adequate instrument to deal with them. As regards the Christian trade unions of Europe, the same considerations applied to their world organization, the International Federation of Christian Trade Unions (CISC), which in its limited sphere was even more oriented toward Europe than the IFTU.

334. During the immediate postwar years the World Federation of Trade Unions made no attempt to regionalize its structure in any part of the world. Thus it was not until after the formation of the ICFTU in 1949 that the first regional grouping for European unions came into existence. This was the ICFTU's European Regional Organization (ERO), founded in 1950, whose affiliates consisted of the European member unions of the ICFTU.

1. The Antecedents of the European Trade Union Confederation

335. The ERO, it must be noted, was not an independent regional body but a subsidiary of the ICFTU. That status, however, in no way diminished its aspiration to become the authoritative regional spokesman for all of Western Europe's trade unions, or at least for the ones that were affiliated with the ICFTU. In pursuit of this aim the ERO staked out a strong claim to be responsible for the coordination of trade union interests vis-à-vis the supranational European agencies that were beginning to emerge during the first phase of integration in the early 1950s.

336. For a few years, the ERO did indeed play that leading role, but already by 1952 it was forced to share its function as regional spokesman with a so-called Committee of Twenty-One. Unlike the more broadly conceived ERO, that Committee was established for a single purpose, namely to secure for its member organizations an influential role in the social and labour policies of the European Coal and Steel Community (ECSC). Accordingly the membership of the Committee of Twenty-One consisted of the seven ICFTU-affiliated trade union federations in the six countries of the Schuman Plan (there were two affiliates from Italy) plus the industrial unions for the coal and steel industries in each one of the countries.

337. Because ERO attempts to have the Committee placed under its overall authority were unsuccessful, the Committee of Twenty-One may be regarded as the first independent European regional trade union body. It was followed on the Christian side in 1955 by the Federation of Christian Trade Unions in the ECSC, although that body cannot be considered as an independent regional organization in view of its integral links with the parent body, the CISC.

338. When the Treaty of Rome created the European Economic Community (EEC) in 1957, the trade unions had to reassess the adequacy of their organizational structure for representing their interests before the comprehensive new agency. The European Regional Organization of the ICFTU expected to become the official coordinating body, but that claim was not acceptable to the national trade union federations in the EEC countries – the 'Six' – because the ERO included among its members a sizable contingent of unions in countries which instead of joining the EEC had decided to found the European Free Trade Association (EFTA) – the 'Seven'. This division among countries and governments spread to the trade unions, and because ERO proved to be too weak to bridge the gulf in the labour sector, the national trade union federations of the 'Six' proceeded to establish their own independent liaison body in 1958. That became the European Trade Union Secretariat which absorbed the

Committee of Twenty-one and assumed general responsibility for the representation of the interests of ICFTU-affiliated trade unions in all the institutions of the Common Market and the Schuman Plan.

339. A parallel responsibility on behalf of the Christian trade unions was after 1958 taken on by the European Organization (EO) of the CISC. At just about the same time the two WFTU affiliates in France and Italy, the CGT and CGIL, set up their own Coordination and Action Committee for the purpose of maintaining liaison on their behalf with the administrative bodies of the EEC. This committee was for several years deliberately ignored by the other trade union groups, for in faithful adherence to general WFTU policies its two constituents had greeted the establishment of supranational European institutions as merely a transparent manoeuvre to shore up the crumbling forces of capitalism. The Italian federation CGIL was the first to abandon this dogmatic view, especially after it became evident that free labour mobility in the Common Market had greatly improved the overall employment prospects for Italian workers in the Community. Nevertheless the political isolation of the Communist labour committee remained in effect until it received official recognition from the European Commission in 1969.

340. It took the unions in the EFTA countries considerably longer than their counterparts in the Common Market to set up a joint trade union lobby. The delay was attributable in part to the looser organization of EFTA itself, as compared with the EEC, and in part to the opposition of the British Trades Union Congress, the key national federation among the EFTA 'Seven'. Thus it was not until 1968 that a Trade Union Committee for the European Free Trade Area (EFTA–TUC) was established, and even then its policy aims and administrative apparatus were modest as measured by the standards established by the unions in the Common Market.

341. During the 1960s the European Trade Union Secretariat became without question the most important of the new European trade union pressure groups. Symbolic of its ambitious perspectives it reorganized itself in 1969 into a European Confederation of Free Trade Unions (ECFTU). Although its constituency remained confined to the ICFTU-affiliated trade union federations in the six Common Market countries, the change in title from Secretariat to the more comprehensive Confederation plus the adoption of new rules and governing structures were clearly intended to signal an interest in expanding its membership.

342. In the ensuing years the ECFTU negotiated repeatedly with the EFTA trade union group and the Christian unions in an effort to consolidate and simplify the complex European trade union structure. These negotiations accelerated once it became likely that Britain and several other countries (but in the end only Denmark and Ireland) would join the Common Market. By the end of 1972 agreement had been reached among all the European ICFTU affiliates to establish an entirely new organization to supersede both the

ECFTU and EFTA–TUC. The door was also kept open for the Christian unions in the WCL, although they were deliberately not included as charter members.

2. The European Trade Union Confederation

343. The founding congress of the new European Trade Union Confederation (ETUC) convened in Brussels in February 1973. In deciding to follow the British lead to omit the word 'free' from the title of the organization – a decision opposed by a minority under West German leadership – some of the founding unions wanted to indicate that membership would not necessarily always be restricted to non-Communist labour organizations. In March 1974, as expected, the Christian trade unions of Europe were admitted as a group and without significant opposition. In July of the same year the Italian CGIL, predominantly under Communist leadership, was also permitted to join, but this time only by a divided vote in which the British TUC led the majority and the German DGB the opposing minority.

344. However, the status of the French CGT still remains in question. The difference in treatment between the Italian and French organizations is based partly on the historically more positive approach of the CGIL toward European unification, partly on the well remembered Stalinist antecedents of contemporary French communism, and partly on the respective state of interunion relations in France and Italy. In Italy, the differences between the affiliates of WFTU and ICFTU have been bridged much more easily than in France. In fact, the three principal Italian labour organizations have repeatedly discussed organic unity, though so far nothing has come of it. In France, however, the ICFTU-affiliated Force Ouvrière has generally refused to have any dealings with the CGT. The third French organization, the CFDT, is ostensibly favourable to admission of the CGT.

345. When the ETUC was established as an independent organization, many of the ICFTU's non-European members feared that their European associates would become preoccupied with intra-European affairs and neglect their worldwide interests and responsibilities. However, the proposed remedy – a formal link between the ICFTU and the ETUC – was unacceptable to the European ICFTU affiliates because of the complications that such an arrangement would have created for the non-ICFTU affiliates in Europe.

346. The two largest affiliates of the ETUC are the British TUC and the West German DGB. Each one has had a turn at the top honour of filling the presidency. On many policy issues there have either been no substantial differences between them, or such differences as do exist have been compromised. On the relatively few occasions when the two have publicly differed the results show no clear pattern. The TUC won the controversy over the title of the organization and subsequently mustered enough support to shoehorn the

Italian CGIL into membership. On the other hand the DGB has successfully blocked the admission of the French CGT, at least until now.

347. The current ETUC general secretary is Mathias Hinterscheid, formerly the president of the Luxemburg trade union federation. He supervises an establishment that services 30 affiliated organizations with a total of 37 million members (as of April 1976). With headquarters conveniently located in Brussels, which is the nearest thing to a European capital, the ETUC has as its principal task the representation of the collective interests of the European trade union movements. Close contacts with the various organs of the European Community are of course essential to the execution of that responsibility, including the coordination of trade union positions in the advisory Economic and Social Committee of the Community.

348. The current main objectives of the ETUC are embodied in a set of resolutions adopted at its Second (London) Congress in April 1976. The demands include, among others,

1. vigorous government action to restore full employment and to forestall a resurgence of inflation (a neat balancing of British and German trade union preoccupations);
2. the extension of industrial democracy through worker participation in company decisions, especially in multinational companies;
3. an integrated European energy policy;
4. a special effort to improve the work environment, including the removal of inequalities that adversely affect women workers, young workers, older workers, migrants and the handicapped; and
5. certain political objectives that are either of very general significance, such as the importance of safeguarding democracy, freedom, detente, security and independence for all European countries, or are more specifically addressed to the situations prevailing in Spain, Portugal, Greece, and Northern Ireland as of April 1976.

349. An account of the ETUC would be incomplete without mentioning the industry committees whose formation is explicitly encouraged by the ETUC constitution. At present there are six such committees at European level. Their coverage includes the metal industries, agriculture, communications, entertainment, white collar occupations, and mining. The general relationship of the committees to the ETUC on one hand and to the International Trade Secretariats on the other remains to be worked out. At present, there are substantial differences from case to case. In the metals industries, for example, the European Metal Workers' Federation constitutes an autonomous organization of the various national unions in these industries. It has its own staff and governing bodies, and though it maintains fraternal relations with the International Metalworkers' Federation, it is in no way subordinate to that more broadly conceived organization. In some other instances, however (for example PTTI and FIET), the European industry committee maintains an organic link with the appropriate International Trade Secretariat, and the two may even share identical full-time officials. It will obviously take time to resolve the overlapping and partly conflicting organizational interests at stake here, and in the end it is quite likely that instead of a single solution several different patterns of relations will entrench themselves.

B. The Americas

350. Independent regional trade unionism probably had its origins in the Western Hemisphere. There the relative isolation from the traditional European centres of international labour created a hospitable environment for autonomous hemispheric labour bodies. The receptiveness was at times decisively reinforced by the will of the American Federation of Labor (AFL) to assume a leadership role in international labour affairs, based on the combined trade union forces of North and South America.

1. The Pan-American Federation of Labor (PAFL)

351. The first hemispheric organization to emerge as a full-fledged independent regional body was the Pan-American Federation of Labor (PAFL). It arose partly out of the shared concerns of the trade union federations in the United States and Mexico over the problems of Mexican worker migration into the United States and partly out of expectations of building up a political climate in Latin America that would be tolerant of free trade unionism. The PAFL was formally established in Laredo, Texas, in November 1917 at a conference attended by delegates from the American Federation of Labor and the recently formed Mexican Confederación Regional Obrera Mexicana, soon to be better known by its initials CROM. PAFL chose as its president Samuel Gompers of the AFL, and as long as he remained at the helm of the AFL in the United States, his support of the Pan-American trade union idea ensured the continuity of the PAFL, although only at a fairly low level of activity. Only a few trade union groups other than those from the U.S. and Mexico ever joined the PAFL, and these came mostly from the Central American and Caribbean areas where the influence of the United States was particularly important.

352. After Gomper's death in 1924 the AFL's commitment to the maintenance of the regional body weakened. PAFL ran into increasing difficulties in reconciling the clashing interests of American and Mexican unions over U.S. immigration policy, and in a departure from its earlier views the AFL declined on several occasions to express opposition to U.S. actions that impinged on the internal affairs of certain Latin American countries. From the late 1920s on, internal differences of mostly an ideological nature led to so many postponements of scheduled PAFL meetings that the organization faded into oblivion. The long-standing attachment of the AFL to a cooperative relationship between capital and labour was, in the end, so far removed from the at least verbally revolutionary goals of most Latin American unions that the gap could simply not be bridged in the long run. The PAFL was never explicitly dissolved, but the desultory wind-up discussion of its affairs at the 1941 AFL convention made clear that, in fact, the organization no longer existed.

353. During its active period the PAFL made at least a nominal contribution to the improvement of relations between the United States and its Latin American neighbours, especially Mexico. It adopted a substantial number of resolutions in support of many conventional and a few not quite so conventional trade union objectives. Among the latter was a demand for labour representation in the diplomatic services of all countries in the Western Hemisphere. On the whole, the imprint of the PAFL on hemispheric trade union relations must be judged to have been limited.

2. Confederación de Trabajadores de América Latina (CTAL)

354. The second significant regional organization for the Western Hemisphere was established in 1938, with Mexico again at the centre. Under the leadership of the Marxist trade union leader Vicente Lombardo Toledano, a breakaway group from the CROM had established a rival Mexican labour federation, the Confederación de Trabajadores de Mexico (CTM). Its relations with the government of President Lazaro Cardenas were extremely close. With the CTM as his nucleus and with the tacit support of his government, Lombardo Toledano in September 1938 convened a well-attended hemispheric trade union meeting in Mexico City from which emerged the new Confederación de Trabajadores de America Latina (CTAL). The new trade union federation in the United States, the Congress of Industrial Organizations (CIO), was represented at this meeting.

355. From its beginnings, CTAL adopted a position on political and economic issues that reflected a strong effort to achieve a coalition of the Popular Front type among the divided trade union groups of Latin America, with room for a variety of ideologies. Soon, however, the organization became closely identified with the views of the international Communist movement in general and the Communist parties of Latin America in particular. For example, in 1939 CTAL characterized the outbreak of the war between Nazi Germany and its opponents as a capitalist-imperialist conflict without interest to the workers of Latin America. However, it reversed that view after the German invasion of the Soviet Union in 1941.

356. During its initial years CTAL could usually count on the backing of the Congress of Industrial Organizations because the domestic competition between the CIO and the AFL over the organization of American workers had spilled over into the international arena. Having been excluded from membership in the International Federation of Trade Unions when the AFL insisted on strict application of the principle of only one affiliate from each country, the CIO regarded its fraternal links with CTAL as a rare opportunity to break out of its isolated position. Ideologically there were no serious obstacles to a CIO relationship with CTAL because during those years the views of a substantial segment of CIO unions coincided more or less with the general line of CTAL. When in 1945 the World Federation of Trade Unions replaced the IFTU as the dominant world labour organization, CTAL was an active participant. Lombardo Toledano attended the founding meetings, and for a number of years the WFTU regarded CTAL as its unofficial regional branch for Latin America.

357. Though successful during the initial years of its existence in attracting widespread support among Latin American trade unions, CTAL's position suffered in the second half of the 1940s. Its steadily closer identification with Communist causes became a serious weakness, especially at the end of the decade when competitive organizations began to contest its preeminence and its *bona fides* as an independent trade union body. During the 1950s CTAL declined even more rapidly in size and standing. Its official dissolution occurred in 1964, but that act was only the confirmation of an already completed demise. CTAL's ideological successor became the so-called Permanent Congress of the Unity of Latin American Workers (CPUSTAL) – at first known as CUTAL – whose close links with the WFTU were already noted at the beginning of this chapter.

3. Confederación Interamericana de Trabajadores (CIT)

358. Efforts to organize a regional body in competition with CTAL began shortly after World War II. The lead in these efforts was taken by the AFL. The AFL's renewed interest in Latin America, dormant during the 1930s, grew out of its postwar decision to undertake a major independent effort in international labour activities throughout the world and particularly in Latin America. Of course that decision, in turn, was a consequence of the AFL's refusal to join in the establishment of the WFTU.

359. With the collaboration of several Latin American unions, including some whose existence was then of recent origin, the AFL in 1948 convened a hemispheric labour congress in Lima, Peru, for the purpose of establishing a new regional labour federation. Calling itself the Confederación Interamericana de Trabajadores (CIT), the new group sought to promote a type of unionism closer to, but not necessarily identical with, the business union ideology of North American labour, and to compete actively for adherents with the WFTU and the CTAL. However, its existence was too brief to allow more than a bare start. The split in the WFTU in 1949 and the resulting formation of the ICFTU later in the same year, an action in which the AFL participated, created an entirely new political and organizational situation for international labour, not only at the world level but also in Latin America. In conformance with the decision of the ICFTU to build up a set of regional organizations, most ICFTU affiliates in North and South America joined forces in 1951 to form the

ICFTU's Latin American regional organization, ORIT. (ORIT is reviewed in the section on the ICFTU's regional organizations.) The CIT was separately represented at the meeting from which ORIT emerged, but since CIT affiliates played from the beginning an important role in ORIT affairs, there was no further need to continue its existence. Consequently CIT dissolved itself.

4. ATLAS

360. Among the first decisions taken by ORIT was a refusal to accept the trade unions of Argentina into membership. These had come under the domination of Juan Perón and his followers in the mid-1940s. After Perón's official accession to power in 1946 Argentina's unions became an instrument for extending Perón's influence throughout Latin America and particularly to promote the Peronist ideology of *Justicialismo*. To this end Perón not only placed labour attaches in Argentine embassies throughout the continent, but he also embarked on the creation of a regional labour federation. From congresses in Asunción, Paraguay (1951) and in Mexico City (1952), there emerged the Agrupación de Trabajadores Latino Americanos Sindicalizados, symbolically abbreviated as ATLAS. Aside from a few well-financed successes in attracting several minority unions from various Latin American countries, including the Mexican CROM, ATLAS failed to establish itself as an influential force in Latin American labour affairs. After Perón's ouster in 1955 the organization ceased its activities since Perón's successor governments in Argentina had no interest in maintaining an expensive but futile operation. There was no formal termination.

C. Africa

361. Despite its relatively late development, trade unionism in Africa has already produced an impressive number of independent regional organizations. Indeed at present there is no other area in the world where the will to maintain an exclusively regional trade union body is as strong as in Africa. This phenomenon is the outcome of several converging factors. In part it is a reaction against past colonial domination that often included organic and hierarchical links between the trade unions of the metropolitan countries and their subsidiary outposts in the colonies. Severance of these links and their replacement by intra-African trade union connections became in most countries a high priority goal after the achievement of national independence.

362. A second consideration reflects the aim of many African governments, based on political or developmental grounds, or both, to eliminate all likely sources of opposition and centres of alternative authority in their countries, including independent trade unions. By compelling the trade unions to terminate their external affiliations with international bodies outside of Africa, the governments have sought to block the flow of financial and ideological support from outside the continent that could sustain an independent and possibly an obstreperous trade union movement. In this perspective a purely Pan-African form of trade unionism has appeared less threatening to the survival of governments than wider and less easily supervised international links.

363. Finally, Africans have also been attracted to the concept of continent-wide unity. Most African states face similar problems of economic, social, and political development. Their sense of a common heritage and a shared destiny, even if unevenly distributed, has helped to promote a regional identification that in spite of rivalries extends to many institutions, including trade union organization.

1. The UGTAN

364. In the French territories of Africa the movement for trade union separation from the French metropolitan and world labour organizations began in the mid-1950s, thus well before the spread of national independence. It culminated in the formation of the *Union Générale des Travailleurs d'Afrique Noire* (UGTAN) in January 1957 at a conference held on Cotonou, Dahomey. The UGTAN drew its membership from the former African affiliates or sections of the French Communist trade union federation, CGT. The condition for affiliation with the UGTAN was severance of ties with the CGT and the World Federation of Trade Unions of which the CGT was then, and still remains today, an important constituent organization.

365. Under the leadership of Sekou Touré of Guinea, the non-aligned UGTAN was at first highly successful in rallying the trade unions of French West Africa around the attainment of Pan-African labour unity. However, after Touré took Guinea out of the French Community in 1958 and promoted an alliance between the UGTAN and the WFTU, the UGTAN lost many of its initial adherents. Some of them joined the ICFTU's African Regional Organization (AFRO) which came into existence in 1960.

366. Although temporarily weakened, the drive for Pan-African labour unity soon gathered new support, well beyond the confines of the Francophonic part of Africa. To an important degree it was directed against the ICFTU's presence in Africa. During the decolonization period the ICFTU had taken a vigorous position in support of the rapid achievement of national independence. Since many African trade unions were linked to national independence movements, this stand together with the offer of financial aid brought a substantial number of African affiliates into the ICFTU. However, the success turned out to be only temporary. The ICFTU did, after all, stand for a form of trade unionism independent of direction by political parties, governments, or other outside forces. This fundamental principle came increasingly into conflict with the efforts of most African governments to achieve an indisputably supreme position in all phases of national existence. Moreover, the ICFTU was broadly identified with Western interests and ideologies at a time when many African states were eager to express their resentments over past injustices and their suspicions over future Western intentions by adopting a neutralist and anti-Western posture. These pressures and currents of ideas lent much support to the promotion of separatist African trade unionism.

2. The All-African Trade Union Federation (AATUF)

367. After preparatory meetings in 1959 and 1960 the constituent congress for a Pan-African trade union body, the All-African Trade Union Federation (AATUF), was held in 1961 in Casablanca. The main issue of contention was dual affiliation with other internationals. One group of trade unions, known as the Casablanca bloc and consisting principally of unions from Ghana, Guinea, Mali, the United Arab Republic, Algeria and Morocco, insisted on the incompatibility of dual links. Another group, called the Monrovia powers and consisting of Nigeria, Ethiopia, Liberia, Sierra Leone, and several unions from French-speaking African states stood for freedom of choice. The separatists won out, and exclusive affiliation with the African organization and none other thus became AATUF's guiding principle. Other positions favoured by AATUF included close ties between trade unions and their governments, the establishment of unitary national trade union federations in all African countries, and hostility toward the West as the embodiment of colonialism, imperialism, and capitalism.

368. From the beginning AATUF established cordial relations with the WFTU. The WFTU's influence in Africa was at that time insignificant. Consequently it had little to lose from AATUF's exclusionist policy, while the ICFTU and to a lesser extent the WCL (or rather its predecessor, the CISC) were highly vulnerable to the appeals of Pan-Africanism. It is, therefore, entirely plausible that the WFTU initially provided generous subsidies to AATUF for its organizational activities.

369. Because of Ghana's key position in the administration of AATUF, the overthrow of the Ghanaian political leader Kwame Nkrumah in 1966 caused serious disruption in the ranks. The Ghanaian general secretary was replaced, and AATUF headquarters were moved from Accra to Dar-es-Salam, Tanzania. At about the same time WFTU subsidies were apparently reduced or even discontinued, and the general effectiveness of AATUF declined considerably.

3. The African Trade Union Confederation (ATUC)

370. The creation of AATUF in 1961 had left those African national trade union centres that favoured freedom of choice sensitive to attacks on grounds of insufficient Pan-African loyalty and subservience to outside interests. In self-defence these organizations, which included affiliates of the ICFTU as well as of the Christian international trade union federation (then still known as the CISC), decided to organize their own purely African regional labour body. This decision was implemented at the 1962 Dakar Conference. The new organization called itself the African Trade Union Confederation (ATUC). Besides advocating freedom of choice in international affiliation, ATUC also favoured trade union independence from government control and a looser and more flexible form of African unity than that favoured by the Casablanca bloc.

371. In the following years, the rivalry between the two organizations – AATUF and ATUC – became keen, though it was usually limited to reciprocal denunciations. AATUF obtained most of its resources from Ghana and probably also from the WFTU with which it entered into close relations. ATUC depended heavily on Senegalese staffing and on ICFTU and WCL material support. Neither organization was in a strong position to offer adequate conventional trade union services to its affiliates. At intervals, both sides agreed to explore the possibility of unification, but conferences in 1963 and 1968 to realize this aim were failures.

4. The Organization of African Trade Union Unity (OATUU)

372. It took government pressure to accomplish what the trade unions were unable, and in some instances no doubt unwilling, to do by themselves. In 1963 the African governments had set up as their own regional body the Organization of African Unity (OAU). In line with its Pan-African objectives the OAU favoured from its very inception a merger of the two African regional trade union organizations, but first it had to overcome tenacious resistance among some of its own member governments which feared that either a united regional labour federation would support radical tendencies among trade unions or else dilute government control over trade unions, or perhaps both. It took almost ten years to allay these concerns and to overcome the reluctance of some of the trade unions themselves, particularly those which wanted to maintain an independent international affiliation. Although that issue was not resolved and indeed has not been satisfactorily settled even now, a founding congress to establish an Organization of African Trade Union Unity (OATUU) was held in April 1973 in Addis Ababa. The OATUU soon superseded both ATUC and AATUF, and it now claims to have in its ranks all the national trade union centres on the African continent, a total at present of 49. Its headquarters are located in Accra, Ghana, and its general secretary is Dennis Akumu, the former general secretary of the Kenyan national trade union centre.

373. In April 1976, three years after its establishment, the OATUU held its second congress in Tripoli, Libya. As revealed on that occasion and already previously during the founding congress in 1973, the general policy line of the OATUU on all issues is patterned closely on the views of the Organization of

African Unity. It subscribes to 'positive neutrality' and non-alignment, and it seeks friendship and fraternal relations with every international trade union organization outside of Africa. In its basic doctrine the OATUU proclaims itself to be anti-capitalist, and it defines its paramount objective to be the struggle 'against imperialism, colonialism, neo-colonialism, racism, zionism, and any form of oppression or exploitation of man'.

374. The question of free choice versus international affiliation was the principal point of contention at the founding congress of the OATUU. It has so remained ever since. Article 8 of the OATUU charter explicitly prohibits dual affiliation. Several affiliates, however, regard that provision as a violation of ILO Convention No. 87 on Freedom of Association and Protection of the Right to Organize. Nevertheless, efforts to amend the objectionable item at the 1976 Tripoli Congress were not put to a vote. Instead the matter was referred to the OATUU Executive Committee which is to report its recommendations to the next congress in 1980.

375. Despite the unambiguous language of the charter, eight OATUU affiliates still retain membership in the ICFTU or WFTU or at least did so at the time of the Tripoli Congress. Most of them are heavily dependent on external aid, but their continued outside links would not be possible without the tacit tolerance of their governments. The International Confederation of Arab Trade Unions (ICATU) is apparently exempt from the prohibition against dual affiliation since a number of African trade union federations belong without hindrance both to OATUU and ICATU.

376. It must be regarded as a major achievement of OATUU international strategy that it has established working relations with all three world trade union bodies – ICFTU, WFTU, and WCL. The substance of the separate relations ranges from high-level joint declarations of principles and policies to the joint operation of labour education programmes in individual countries. Separate consultations between the OATUU and the three international federations take place on a regular basis, and reciprocal representation at major functions such as trade union congresses has become customary. These neatly balanced relationships express, on one hand, a successful implementation of OATUU policies to maintain fraternal relations with all international organizations and represent, on the other hand, an effort by the ICFTU, WFTU, and WCL to keep an African foothold, even if a narrow and uncomfortable one. But there is another element as well. Just as in virtually all African countries the trade unions must take policy guidance from their governments, so the OATUU must pay due attention to the views of the (intergovernmental) Organization of African Unity. By entering into parallel relations with several international trade union bodies the OATUU manages at least to a small degree to diminish its otherwise almost complete political dependence on the OAU. Moreover, joint ventures and programmes with other international bodies enable the OATUU to engage in and take credit for activities that its own resources could probably not support.

377. In this connection it should be noted that the financial affairs of the OATUU are as inscrutable as are those of the WFTU and the WCL. The official affiliation fee is $3,000 per year for each affiliated organization regardless of size. Whether this obligation is always met – which is highly doubtful in any case – and from which source the contributions are actually derived are questions that cannot be answered on the basis of available information. The report of the OATUU Financial Committee at the Tripoli Congress urged 'more strictness in the use of the funds put at the disposal of the organization' and emphasized 'the vital necessity of financing the OATUU activities by contributions from the affiliates only'. Clearly there are important implications in these strictures, but the report did not spell out the specific reasons which led to them.

378. The accent of OATUU concerns rests heavily on political and international issues and more lightly on the social and labour policies of individual African countries. Unlike its regional counterparts in Latin America and Western Europe, the OATUU does not generally express views that are critical of the acts of African governments. Nor could it afford to do so. Against a background of universal and far-reaching government intervention in trade union affairs the Tripoli Congress cautiously limited itself to recommend earnestly to the various African governments that they respect trade union freedom and democracy as stipulated in ILO Conventions. Anything more outspoken would not be tolerated. It is also revealing that in a situation where in most countries the governments are themselves the largest employers, OATUU criticism of unfair labour and employment practices is generally confined to the (private) employers of migrant African workers in Western Europe and more generally to multinational companies.

D. The Middle East

379. In 1956, a congress of trade unions from several Arab countries met in Damascus on the initiative of the Jordanian Federation of Labour Unions to found the International Confederation of Arab Trade Unions (ICATU). The dominant role was soon taken by Egypt whose international policies were at that time determined by the pan-Arabic and worldwide ambitions of President Nasser. ICATU headquarters were set up in Cairo, an Egyptian was designated as general secretary, and Egyptian government funds very likely were a chief support of ICATU expenditures.

380. At the outset ICATU formulated its principal task to be the mobilization of workers and their organizations in the struggle for Arab unity. Believing that external forces were chiefly responsible for preventing that unity, ICATU directed its publicity particularly against the vestiges of colonialism and imperialism in the Middle East and also, of course, against Zionism.

381. For many years the preeminent position of Egypt determined the views of IACTU on whatever issues came before it, including relations with other international labour bodies. Officially ICATU's general posture was one of non-alignment between East and West. Nevertheless, relations with the WFTU were most of the time far closer than those with the ICFTU. The reason was that the WFTU was willing and indeed eager to give all-out public support to the Arab side in the conflict with Israel, whereas the ICFTU's cautiously worded appeals for a peaceful and lasting Middle Eastern settlement through negotiations appeared to the Arabs to constitute one-sided support of Israeli interests. (The suspicion of ICFTU partiality was undoubtedly reinforced by the knowledge that the Israeli Labour organization Histadrut was and is an important ICFTU constituent.)

382. Recent political changes in the Middle East following on President Sadat's peace initiative late in 1977 will to some extent test ICATU's stamina. Its headquarters have already been moved temporarily from Cairo to Baghdad, an Iraqi national has become general secretary, and at least for the time being Egyptian hegemony has ended. In the past ICATU's internal cohesiveness has been greatest during periods of intensified Arab conflict with Israel and weakest during periods of detente. It is therefore quite safe to conclude that until relations between the several Arab countries have sorted themselves out, ICATU will be dependent even more than before on political guidance and financial support from governments that continue to regard it as a useful body.

II. Specialized Functional Organizations

383. One of the most important international developments in the post-World War II period has been the creation of interest communities among countries that are linked to one another by geographic proximity, degree of industrialization, shared political values, or some combination of these factors. The outstanding example is, of course, the European Common Market, but it is by no means the only one. By and large, trade unions have strongly supported the creation of such communities, certainly in the Western world. They regard them as engines of economic advancement, mediators of international disputes, and models of gradually expanding supranational administration. In return for their support, the trade unions have asked for, and have generally received, recognition as the legitimate representatives of the views of wage earners before these agencies on issues that are of special concern to working men and women.

A. The OECD Trade Union Advisory Committee (TUAC)

384. One of the most important intergovernmental agencies is the Organization for Economic Cooperation and Development (OECD). It is the successor to the Organization for European Economic Cooperation (OEEC) that was originally created in 1948 to coordinate the individual national recovery programmes of the European countries sharing in Marshall Plan aid. Instead of simply abandoning the OEEC when its task had been completed the member governments decided in 1961 to reformulate its objectives, enlarge its membership, and make an appropriate alteration in the title of the organization. As revised, the chief purposes of the new OECD became the promotion of economic growth, employment, and living standards under conditions of financial stability; the expansion of economic assistance to developing countries; and the stimulation of world trade on a multilateral and non-discriminatory basis. The membership was enlarged beyond the original group of European Marshall Plan countries by including the United States, Canada, and Japan.

385. Ever since the early beginnings of OECD's predecessor organization in 1948, the trade unions have contributed to the work of the agency through a Trade Union Advisory Committee (TUAC). In the initial years of the Marshall Plan, TUAC helped to mobilize the support of European workers for the recovery programme over Communist opposition and in the face of widespread scepticism about basic American intentions. The success of this effort earned TUAC the respect of hard-pressed governments, and the committee came to be viewed as a useful and constructive pressure group. Subsequently its prestige rose even further because of its contribution to the success of productivity improvement programmes designed to restore the international competitive position of the war-shattered European economies.

386. By including in its constituency not only the numerically dominant socialist trade union federations of Europe but also the smaller Christian organizations, TUAC was able to avoid the kind of embroilment in national trade union rivalries that often spills over into international agencies. Its comprehensiveness strengthened its claim of being representative of the vast majority of wage earners in the OEEC countries – and subsequently the OECD countries.

387. At present TUAC includes slightly over 30 trade union organizations from twenty OECD countries, including all the principal European ones except for the French CGT and the Italian CGIL, the labour federations in Canada and the United States (which rejoined in July 1976), and the second largest Japanese federation, DOMEI. Almost all these groups are affiliated internationally with the ICFTU or WCL, and consequently there is generally a close working relationship between TUAC on one side and these two international trade union federations and the fraternally associated International Trade Secretariats on the other.

388. TUAC headquarters are located in Paris. The governing structure provides for a plenary body that includes all affiliates and a smaller Administrative Committee that oversees the budget and personnel policies. Separate working parties are formed to deal with special issues. The secretariat of about six persons is headed by a general secretary, currently Kari Tapiola, an ex-staff member of the Finnish SAK. He and his associates operate under the general direction of a General Council of TUAC affiliates. The work of the secretariat is financed by member contributions of currently 14 French francs (about $3.50) per 1,000 members. It may be estimated very roughly that the annual budget amounts to about $250,000.

389. OECD is not in the first instance an 'action' agency but is concerned more with producing objective information and expert advice and recommendations for the policy guidance of member governments. The general excellence and objectivity of OECD reports, studies, and recommendations have conferred on the agency a wide measure of respect among the most diverse groups. The greater the esteem enjoyed by the OECD and the stronger the likelihood of having its recommendations accepted, the more important it is for the trade unions to ensure consideration for the views of their constituents. After all, they will have to live with the consequences. In general, therefore, TUAC seeks to inject a trade union perspective into issues under consideration at OECD and ultimately to get its perspective included as far as possible in the substance of OECD reports and recommendations.

390. Among OECD issues of particular concern to TUAC have been the incomes and employment policies of the member governments, the setting of overall economic growth objectives, the achievement of industrial and economic democracy through worker participation in management, manpower policies and human resource development schemes, economic aid to less developed countries, international trade and tariff policies, and most recently the burgeoning area of international controls over the activities of multinational companies.

391. OECD was the first international agency to set voluntary guidelines for the conduct of multinational companies. These were adopted in June 1976 after having passed through a long series of preliminary drafts and reviews. TUAC and its counterpart on the employer side (the Business and Industry Advisory Committee) took an active part in the process. The final version had TUAC's endorsement, though it was given with some reluctance because the unions had hoped for more comprehensive and more stringent rules. In order to correct these shortcomings TUAC has coordinated a number of efforts designed to persuade the relevant OECD bodies and the member governments of the need for meticulous supervision of the guidelines and ultimately of the importance of adopting stricter controls.

392. As a general rule the work performed by TUAC is not of a spectacular character. It rarely creates headlines, and there have been occasions when the TUAC Secretariat has had to make a special effort to justify to its constituent labour federations the importance of its continued existence. But though it may not be easily visible, the work is nevertheless of considerable importance since the consultative relationship with the OECD constitutes one of the few opportunities for trade unions to exert influence on the shaping of economic and social policies at international level.

B. COSATE

393. Functionally similar to TUAC is the role of the Trade Union Technical Advisory Council (COSATE) in the inter-American labour system. COSATE's assigned tasks are to advise the Inter-American Conference of Ministers of Labour, the Permanent Technical Committee on Labour Matters (COTPAL), and the appropriate administrative departments of the Secretariat of the Organization of American States on the initiation and execution of programmes of special concern to workers and to ensure their participation in development activities at national and regional levels. In its present form, COSATE was established by the Third Conference of Labour Ministers in 1969 as the successor body to a similar organ of older vintage.

394. The membership of COSATE consists of the trade union organizations of the Latin American countries and the United States. Most but not all of the members are affiliates of the ICFTU's Inter-American organization, ORIT. None belongs to the WCL's Latin American body, CLAT. Unlike its TUAC counterpart at the Organization for Economic Cooperation and Development, COSATE has no independent income. It depends financially on allocations from the budget of the Organization of American States (OAS), and as a general rule that kind of dependency tends to be a sign of weakness rather than of strength. To the extent that COSATE's activities require continuity in the three-year intervals between meetings of the Inter-American Conference of Ministers of Labour, it is provided by a nine-member provisional executive committee established in 1975.

Affiliates of the European Trade Union Confederation (ETUC)

Country	Organization	Membership (1 April 1978)
Austria	Oesterreichischer Gewerkschaftsbund (ÖGB)	1,600,000
Belgium	Fédération Générale du Travail de Belgique (FGTB)	900,000
	Confédération des Syndicats Chrétiens de Belgique (CSC)	1,100,000
Denmark	Landsorganisationen i Danmark (LO)	990,000
	Faellerstradet for Danske Tjenestemandsog Funktionaerorganisationer (FTF)	240,000
Finland	Toimihenkilö-ja Virkamiesjärjestöjen Keskuslitto (TVK)	240,000
	Suomen Ammattilittojen Keskusjärjestö (SAK)	920,000
France	Confédération Générale du Travail-Force Ouvrière (CGT-FO)	1,000,000

Country	Organization	Membership (1 April 1978)
	Confédération Française Démocratique du Travail	900,000
Germany	Deutscher Gewerkschaftsbund (DGB)	6,800,000
Great Britain	Trades Union Congress	10,000,000
Greece	Greek General Confederation of Labor (GSEE)	300,000
Iceland	Althydusamband Islands (ASI)	42,000
Ireland	Irish Congress of Trade Unions (KCTU)	547,000
Italy	Confederazione Italiana Sindicati Lavoratori (CISL)	2,500,000
	Confederazione Generale Italiana del Lavoro (CGIL)	4,500,000
	Unione Italiana del Lavoro (UIL)	800,000
Luxemburg	Confédération Générale de Travail du Luxembourg (CGT)	32,000
	Luxemburgischer Christlicher Gewerkschaftsbund (LCGB)	15,000
Malta	General Workers Union (GWU)	26,000
Netherlands	Nederlands Verbond van Vakverenigingen (NVV)	701,000
	Nederlands Katholiek Vakverbond (NKV)	339,000
	Christelijk Nationaal Vakverbond (CNV)	207,000
Norway	Landsorganisajonen i Norge (LO)	680,000
Spain	Union General de Trabajadores de Espana (UGT)	35,000
	Solidaridad de Trabajadores Vascos (STV)	15,000
Sweden	Landsorganisationen i Sverige (LO)	1,751,000
	Tjänstemännens Centralorganisation (TCO)	922,000
Switzerland	Schweizerischer Gewerkschaftsbund (SGB)	475,000
	Christlich-Nationaler Gewerkschaftsbund (CGS)	106,000
	Schweizerischer Verband Evangelischer Arbeiter und Angestellten (SVEA)	14,000
	Total	38,700,000

Affiliates of the Trade Union Advisory Committee to the Organization for Economic Cooperation and Development (TUAC-OECD)

Australia	Australian Council of Trade Unions (ACTU)
Austria	Oesterreichischer Gewerkschaftsbund (ÖGB)
Belgium	Fédération Générale du Travail de Belgique (FGTB)
	Confédération des Syndicats Chrétiens de Belgique (CSC)
Canada	Canadian Labour Congress (CLC)
	Confederation of National Trade Unions (CSN/CNTO)
Denmark	Landsorganisation i Danmark (Danish Federation of Trade Unions (LO)
	Faellerstrådet for danske Tjenestemandsog Funktionaer-organisationer (FTF) (Federation of Danish Civil Servants and Salaried Employees Organizations)
Finland	Suomen Ammattilittojen Keskusjärjestö (SAK) (Central Organization of Finnish Trade Unions)
France	Confédération Française Démocratique du Travail (CFDT)
	Confédération Générale du Travail-Force Ouvrière (CGT-FO)
	Confédération Générale des Cadres (CGC)
	Fédération de l'Education Nationale (FEN)
Great Britain	Trades Union Congress (TUC)
Germany	Deutscher Gewerkschaftsbund (DGB)
Greece	Greek General Confederation of Labour (GSEE)
Iceland	Althydusamband Islands (Icelandic Federation of Labour) (ASI)
Ireland	Irish Congress of Trade Unions (ICTU)
Israel	General Federation of Labour in Eretz Israel (HISTADRUT)
Italy	Confederazione Italiana Sindicati Lavoratori (Italian Federation of Labour) (CISL)
Japan	Japanese Confederation of Labour (DOMEI)
Luxemburg	Confédération Générale de Travail du Luxembourg (CGT)
	Luxemburgischer Christlicher Gewerkschaftsbund (LCGB)
Netherlands	Confederation Netherlands Trade Union Movement (FNV)
	Christelijk Nationaal Vakverbond (Protestant National Trade Union Federation) (CNV)
Norway	Landsorganisajonen i Norge (Norwegian Federation of Trade Unions) (LO)
Spain	Union General de Trabajadores de España (UGT)
Sweden	Landsorganisationen i Sverige (Swedish Confederation of Trade Unions) (LO)
	Tjänstemännens Centralorganisation (Swedish Central Organization of Salaried Employees) (TCO)
Switzerland	Schweizerischer Gewerkschaftsbund (SGB)
	Christlich-Nationaler Gewerkschaftsbund (CGS)

Affiliates of the Trade Union Advisory Committee to the Organization for Economic Cooperation and Development (TUAC-OECD)

	Schweizerischer Verband Evangelischer Arbeiter und Angestellten (SVEA)
United States	American Federation of Labor-Congress of Industrial Organizations (AFL-CIO)

Chapter VIII. International Trade Secretariats

1. Organization and Structure

395. Less prominent than the international groupings of national trade union federations (ICFTU, WFTU, WCL) but in certain respects of at least equal and possibly greater significance are those organizations that are composed of individual unions in a given industrial sector. Such industrial internationals, as they may be called, are associated in one form or another with all three of the global internationals. The ICFTU maintains a continuing and generally close relationship with 16 organizations of this kind, collectively known as the International Trade Secretariats (ITSs). The WFTU has under its wing 11 roughly corresponding bodies to whom the overall designation Trade Union Internationals (TUIs) has been given. (At an earlier time they were called International Trade Departments.) The WCL contains a similar group of 12 International Trade Federations. All three sets of organizations are listed in an annex to this chapter.

A. Industrial and Global Internationals

396. The terms of the linkage between global and industrial internationals differ substantially from one grouping to another. Consequently, so does the status of the industrial internationals. Taking them in the same order as above, the ITSs are in every respect autonomous bodies whose association with the ICFTU is voluntary and fraternal. The financial resources of the ITSs are furnished directly and entirely by their own affiliates, except in the case of one or two organizations whose financial weakness requires an ICFTU subsidy. The internal government and policy making of the ITSs are wholly their own affair, although they have voluntarily assumed an obligation to stay within the ICFTU's general policies.

397. The 11 TUIs, by contrast, constitute an integral part of the WFTU and are ultimately subject to the WFTU's supervision. Moreover, their financial support is allocated to them by the WFTU which is reported to distribute approximately 25 per cent of its own income from affiliation fees among them. Although since 1969 the TUIs seem to have been given a certain degree of internal self-government, they are not autonomous organizations. That is, they are not able to determine their goals and activities without close reference to the WFTU's overall position on major policy issues. Indeed, the WFTU maintains a headquarters department exclusively for the TUIs.

398. Each TUI has its own bylaws and governing structure. As a rule each one is presided over by an administrative committee headed by a president and several vice presidents. These offices are honorific, and care is taken to ensure that insofar as possible they are filled by the leaders of unions from both Communist and Western countries. The full-time employees in the various secretariats work under the direction of a general secretary. Most TUIs have their central office in the WFTU headquarters building in Prague, but a few are scattered about in other Eastern European capitals. One is located in Helsinki.

399. The International Trade Federations of the WCL are so small and weak that they depend for their sustenance and continuity almost entirely on the WCL. Currently their status is under review, as mandated by the WCL's 1977 Congress, and one conceivable outcome among several alternatives is the dissolution of all or some of the Federations. Should that occur, it is probable that many member unions wil seek admission to the ITS appropriate to their industry. Several national unions affiliated with the French CFDT have already been admitted to the appropriate ITS or are seeking affiliation. Such cross-affiliation has also occured among Dutch national unions in the confessional federations affiliated with the WCL.

400. Except as noted below, there are virtually no relations between the three sets of industrial internationals, although informal contacts may occur from time to time, particularly within the framework of meetings of the ILO's Industrial Committees. An exception is constituted by a 1972 agreement on cooperation that links three ITSs operating in the public sector – the PSI, PTTI, and IFFTU – with two counterparts among the WCL's International Trade Federations, namely the INFEDOP and WCT. Their cooperation covers joint action in the ILO and other international bodies and also extends to intra-European matters. It also includes an undertaking not to have any contacts with the WFTU or any of its organs.

401. Because of the unfortunate paucity of information available on the WFTU's Trade Union Internationals and the WCL's International Trade Federations, and because of the largely subordinate status of their existence, the ensuing account will concentrate on the International Trade Secretariats. As a group they are by far the most important and most active international organizations of their kind, and a few of them operate an impressive establishment.

B. Relationship Between ITSs and ICFTU

402. International Trade Secretariats exist primarily to advance the collective interests of their member unions as the representatives of employees in the industries and occupations over which they exercise jurisdiction. Since their mandate is primarily an 'industrial' rather than a 'political' one, the ITSs devote virtually all of their resources to services and activities that in one way or another help to support the bargaining, legislative, and related interests of their constituents. Their relationship with the ICFTU thus implies a certain division of labour within the general community of interests that links them together.

1. The Milan Agreement

403. In a formal sense the relationship is a voluntary association based, as already noted, on the terms of the 'Milan Agreement' of 1951, as revised by the 1969 ICFTU Congress. The agreement commits the ITSs to follow the general policy of the ICFTU on major policy issues. It further defines the relationship by specifying the right of the secretariats to be represented by non-voting members or delegates in the governing bodies of the ICFTU: congress, executive board, and subcommittees. The agreement also commits the ICFTU to recognize the General Conference of the ITSs as the collective representative of the ITSs, but this commitment does not preclude the ICFTU from simultaneously maintaining bilateral relations with individual ITSs.

404. That there is a basic identity of views between the two sides should not be surprising in view of the fact that both derive their membership essentially from constituencies which share a similar conception of the basic role of trade unions. But since their compact depends entirely on voluntary adherence, not all of the differences that are inevitable in such an arrangement – whether for personality or for institutional reasons – have always been easily resolved. On certain occasions one or another ITS has chosen to follow its own line on a given issue; and if the matter has been of sufficiently great importance, the exercise of autonomy may have led to a temporary or even a lasting breach of relations.

405. Differences over membership criteria have been one of the friction points between the ICFTU and the ITSs, though acute problems have not occurred often. One instance was the decision in the mid-1960s by the International Graphical Federation to admit a French printing trades union which was, and still is, affiliated domestically with the Communist-led CGT. The vote to admit was close, the arguments inside the IGF itself were acrimonious, and two IGF member unions on the losing side disaffiliated in protest. The ICFTU regarded the admission of the French union as a violation of the Milan Agreement, while the IGF stood on its right of internal autonomy. A long break in relations followed, but it has recently been healed. The affair confirmed what was already well known, namely, that the ICFTU cannot impose its will on an ITS under present arrangements.

406. Occasionally proposals for substantial changes in relations are advanced, but so far without effect. A few years ago, for example, some officials of the Norwegian LO suggested a more centralized arrangement under which the ITSs would have become administrative departments of the ICFTU. The idea collapsed when it became evident that there was no support among the ITSs.

2. The ITS General Conference

407. The principle of autonomy governs not only the relations between the ICFTU and the ITSs but also among the ITSs themselves. Of course, the ITSs do have many interests and problems in common, and in order to discuss and to resolve them they have for many years met from time to time, usually once a year, in their own General Conference. The ICFTU has been represented at these gatherings by its top officials. A recurrent topic of discussion at these meetings has been the strengthening of contacts between ICFTU and ITSs. During certain periods, usually when for some reason sharp differences with the ICFTU have arisen, the ITSs have maintained – in addition to the General Conference – a standing liaison body of their own. But at present the General Conference constitutes the only formal link among the ITSs. Informal contracts are, of course, an almost daily occurrence among the ITSs and between them and the ICFTU.

C. Membership

408. Just as there is enormous variation in the size and structure of unions within a given country, so there is bound to be a wide diversity in the membership of the several ITSs. The membership data in the table at the end of this chapter must be regarded, of course, with caution since at least some of the organizations are likely to have inflated their reports for the same reasons that lead global internationals to do so. A contrary tendency, i.e. underreporting of membership, may also occur but is less common. Almost invariably it would be the result of purely financial considerations, particularly in the case of those ITSs whose affiliation fees are fixed in appreciating currencies, such as the Swiss franc.

409. Nowadays well over half of all ITSs have three million members or more. In 1927, only three ITSs out of 26 had as many as one million members. The largest organization by a wide margin is the International Metalworkers' Federation (IMF), followed by the Commercial and Clerical Workers (FIET by its French initials), Public Service Employees (PSI), Chemical Workers (ICEF), Textile Workers (ITGLWF), and Transport Workers (ITF). At one time the ITF had led all other Secretariats in size, but shifts in the industrial and occupational structure across many countries have created a new rank order and have sharply diminished some organizations, for example the miners, while boosting others, (In 1954, the Miners' Secretariat still claimed 2,700,000 members instead of its current 1,200,000.) As is to be expected, the 'growth sectors' among the ITSs run generally parallel with developments in the national economies of the industrialized countries and include among others the public sector and the service trades.

410. Europe and North America provide the bulk of ITS membership, but most ITSs attract a following from all areas of the world, except where Communist governments are in power. Certain ITSs have been able to gain affiliates in countries where the government has prevented the national trade union centres from affiliating with an international confederation. The distinction is an interesting one. Because the ICFTU, WFTU, and WCL are perceived as organizations with an explicit ideological commitment, certain governments, particularly those anxious to appear as nonaligned or seeking to exclude foreign influence, do not allow their national trade union federations to enter into alliances that may carry political implications. Such governments may, however, be more tolerant about the affiliation of an individual union with one of the ITSs because they are regarded as essentially non-political organizations. Thus the overlap of membership between the ITSs and the ICFTU, which was once very close, has now diminished to the point where in some ITSs a substantial portion of affiliated organizations has no ties on its home grounds with the ICFTU-affiliated national centre. There is, however, also another reason. American unions contribute an important component of many ITSs, but their national centre, the AFL-CIO does not belong to the ICFTU.

D. Jurisdiction and Consolidation

411. It ought to be noted that the demarcation lines of the various ITSs do not necessarily coincide with the lines that separate one union from another in a given country. In fact, such areas of jurisdiction vary a great deal from one country to another. However, it appears that the overall ITS structure does correspond fairly closely to the industrial structure of the German and Austrian trade union movements. In such a structure, disputes over demarcation lines are not likely to occur with the same frequency that one would expect from the highly mixed and diffuse structure of Anglo-Saxon trade unionism.

412. The principal jurisdictional dispute, one which lasted for a number of years, involved overlapping membership claims between the International Federation of Petroleum and Chemical Workers (IFPCW) and the International Federation of Chemical, Energy, and General Workers Unions (ICEF). After the collapse of merger negotiations, the IFPCW suspended its operations as of about 1974–75, but has not yet formally dissolved itself. Some of its affiliates joined the ICEF. Others, however, notably the oil workers unions in Latin America, refused to do so.

413. Although many ITSs originally started out as organizations covering a single industry or occupation, they have gradually become multi-industrial or multi-sectoral bodies. This development has come about partly through amalgamation and partly through extension into newly developed economic sectors. Nowadays virtually every ITS cuts across two or more industrial branches. For example, the International Metalworkers' Federation covers the basic steel, automobile manufacturing, shipbuilding, machinery (including electrical and electronic), and aerospace industries, plus other industrial branches that are included within these major groups such as the huge sector which in Britain is called the engineering industries. Similarly, the membership of the International Transport Workers' Federation is spread across rail, road, air, seafaring and inland water transport, and also includes fisheries and stevedoring. FIET, the second largest ITS, is a multi-sectoral organization of employees' unions in banking, insurance, commerce and industry. Often the very title of the organization reveals its composite origins, as for instance in the case of the Textile, Garment and Leather Workers' Secretariat.

1. Trade Groups

414. Considerations of cost savings and efficiency have been of primary importance in stimulating these internal consolidations, just as has been the case in union mergers at national level. The resulting expansion in size and reach and the accumulation of industrial sectors within a single organization have compelled many ITSs to establish administrative subdivisions to cater to the distinct needs of the various branches. Many composite national unions have, of course, followed the same pattern so as to provide proper services geared to the varying needs of members spread out over several different industries. In the ITSs, the administrative subdivisions are generally known as trade groups or trade sections. Where their existence is linked to a merger of previously independent organizations, they are likely to correspond to the contours of the participants in the merger. For example, the three trade sections of the Textile, Garment, and Leather Workers' Federation follow exactly the lines of the three formerly separate parts of that organization.

2. Corporation Councils

415. Another administrative innovation, though structurally different from departmentalization by industry, has been the establishment of corporation councils that are designed to parallel the largest employers of ITS members. This development will be reviewed below in conjunction with the subject of ITS strategy toward multinational companies.

3. Regionalization

416. Regionalization in the form of subordinate regional structures for the major areas of the world constitutes yet another ITS effort to stay administratively abreast of the problems inherent in large-scale organizations. The process has gone further in the European area than elsewhere, but not without causing some concerns. The European Trade Union Confederation (ETUC) has encouraged the creation of European industry committees, provided that these committees operate under the ETUC's general aegis. But this arrangement is considered unsatisfactory by several ITSs. That explains why in the PTTI and FIET the general secretaries have assumed the additional responsibility of administering the affairs of their European regional committees. That arrangement, for two out of the current total of eight regional industry committees, is designed to ensure the European region's continuing and close attachment to the ITS central office. On the other hand, in the very important metals sector the European Metalworkers' Federation leads an entirely autonomous existence under a general secretary and staff of its own. However, the presidency of IMF and the vice presidency of EMF are currently held by the same individual – Eugen Loderer, the head of the German Metalworkers' Union.

417. The differences are not only bureaucratically motivated but also involve policy issues. For instance, the autonomous ETUC expects all European industry committees to adopt ETUC rather than ITS membership criteria. Because the ETUC's membership is made up of national centres affiliated with the ICFTU as well as the WCL, and also includes the Italian CGIL which was until recently affiliated with the WFTU, the clear implication is that the European industry committees ought to accept not only ICFTU-connected affiliates but also WCL and perhaps even WFTU affiliates. Most ITSs, however, still confine their membership to unions whose national centres are ICFTU affiliates, or at least to unions whose ideological views place them within the ICFTU family, and they are under strong pressure from powerful member organizations, especially their American affiliates, to maintain this policy.

418. Another policy gap between ETUC and ITSs stems from built-in differences over the proper strategy to be adopted vis-à-vis the multinationals. In this respect the predisposition of several ITSs, and certain national unions such as the Dutch Industriebond (NVV), is to erect inter-union structures on a company-by-company basis – the so-called corporation councils or variants thereof – and to formulate a programme of action centered on the attainment of collective bargaining rights and international legislative or quasi-legislative regulation. The ETUC's essentially regional perspective, however, tends to produce an inevitable emphasis on Community-wide rather than broader global approaches, as for example the adoption of a European company statute. These are not insuperable differences, but unless properly managed they produce frictions and exacerbate rivalries that diminish the effectiveness of the organizations concerned.

E. Governing Bodies

419. In their internal government the ITSs have developed too much diversity for fully valid generalizations. Nevertheless there are sufficient similarities among most of them to create a general pattern.

420. As a rule, the congresses hold supreme legislative power to elect the top officers, notably the general secretary. They also set the financial obligations. Most often they meet triennially. Voting rights are usually distributed in proportion to paid-up membership.

421. Given the industrial interests of ITSs, the business sessions of the congresses are predominantly devoted to discussions of ways of protecting and improving the terms and conditions of employment in the relevant industrial sectors. Political questions are not necessarily excluded. On occasion they may even become very prominent. But as a rule they take a back seat because in most ITSs the member organizations are in general agreement on fundamental political issues.

422. There are, however, exceptions. One such exception occurred at the 1976 Helsinki Congress of FIET, the white-collar employees' secretariat. That congress adopted a resolution which condemned totalitarian regimes in general but singled out the Chilean military government. FIET's American affiliates considered the terms of the resolution to be excessively preoccupied with Chile in particular and Latin America in general. Following the congress they reappraised for several months their ties with FIET while their seats on FIET's executive board remained ostentatiously vacant. Eventually the difference was settled when the FIET executive board adopted a broad-gauged resolution supporting the efforts of Amnesty International on behalf of political prisoners everywhere. On this basis the American unions then agreed to resume their seats.

423. In many ITSs there used to be a general council which because of its smaller size than the congress could meet more frequently and at less expense. Its tasks and authority were defined in terms similar to those of the congress, and its representativeness of the constituency as a whole was approximately the same as that of the congress. For reasons of economy, however, general councils have been disappearing from the governing bodies of the ITSs, thereby increasing the significance of the executive bodies.

424. Of overriding importance in the hierarchy of ITS governing bodies is the executive committee, though that is not always the name given to it. Its composition tends to be fairly small, about a dozen members or less, and for obvious reasons most seats are reserved for the largest, wealthiest, and most influential affiliates. Because the organizations which fit these attributes are almost invariably Western European, North American, or Japanese, several ITSs have made provisions in recent years – some voluntarily, some under pressure – to ensure wider regional representation on executive boards. In some instances regional conferences instead of the triennial congresses now select the members of the executive body, but these efforts to diversify have not always gone far enough to satisfy all the unions from Third World countries.

425. To supplement the executive committee several ITSs have established an even smaller management committee. For instance the Building and Woodworkers with a 17-member executive board have designated a five-member management committee which can meet with sufficient frequency to give continuing policy direction to top staff officials. Similarly in the International Transport Workers' Federation a four-member committee drawn from affiliated unions in the country where ITS headquarters are located (Great Britain) supervises the day-to-day operations of the secretariat.

F. Secretariat

426. The term 'secretariat' designates not only each one of the several ITSs but also, and somewhat confusingly, the permanent office that in each instance is in operational charge. Invariably the secretariat is headed by a general secretary, and he is always the key official. Before World War II and in some instances even for several years afterwards most ITS general secretaries were able to perform their functions on a part-time basis, aided perhaps by one or two clerk-typists and a translator. The balance of their time they devoted to the affairs of their own national body which probably paid most of their salary. Nowadays, however, virtually all general secretaries are expected to be full-time officials. In the larger organizations they head up a sizable establishment which may include one or more assistant general secretaries, research officers, field representatives, translators, and the usual complement of support staff. In the smaller ones, more modest circumstances prevail.

427. With a single exception, ITS headquarters have always been located in a European country. (The exception is, or rather was, the International Federation of Petroleum and Chemical Workers which until its demise had its main office in Denver, Colorado.) Before 1933 Germany was the preferred location, partly because of its centrality and partly because German unions were often the largest affiliates and the chief financial contributors. Subsequently Great Britain took Germany's place for some years as the most commonly chosen headquarters site.

428. In the last few years the consolidation and growth of the ITSs have enabled them to become increasingly independent of the support and influence of a single major affiliate. Consequently, or at least concurrently, there has been an important change in the criteria for chosing the seat of the organization. Of chief importance now is proximity to inter-governmental agencies engaged in tasks important to the ITSs. Almost half of all ITSs, seven to be exact, have established themselves in Geneva, Switzerland, where they have ready access to the International Labour Office, can easily participate in ILO activities, and can also stay in close touch with each other. Three have settled in Brussels which, of course, houses not only the European Economic Community but also the International Confederation of Free Trade Unions and the World Confederation of Labour. Three still remain in or near London. The others are scattered about.

G. Finances

429. The financial arrangements of the ITSs are far too diverse to be reviewed here except in very broad outlines. With only one or two exceptions, as noted below, they all derive their normal operating funds entirely from their own affiliates. The actual amount of the levy tends to depend mostly on whether an ITS operates in a high or low wage industry. The actual amount collected also depends on the ability to pay of affiliates. In the case of the IMF, to cite just one case, the affiliation fee was set in 1974 at 50 Swiss centimes per member per year, a fairly typical figure. This should have yielded approximately 6.5 million Swiss francs on a total membership claim of 13 million. But the amount actually collected was only 2.7 million Swiss francs. The explanation for the apparent discrepancy has general application. Affiliates in less developed countries are automatically exempted from that portion of the dues which is allocated to the IMF's International Solidarity Fund, which is about half the amount due. In addition, a number of these unions were granted a still lower rate, in some cases down to zero. With other sources of income added, mostly from returns of investments, total IMF income for 1976 came to about 3.4 million Swiss francs – still an impressive amount and as of that time probably the highest annual income ever received by an ITS.

430. For some ITS affiliates, even those in wealthy industrialized countries, the size of the affiliation fee can become a significant burden. When in 1969 the IFBWW raised its affiliation fee to 50 Swiss centimes per member per year, its British affiliates opposed the decision and subsequently disaffiliated, not in anger but in penury. (As of 1980 the rate is 0.90 Swiss francs per member per year.) The recent decline in the dollar has caused problems even for the American affiliates of several ITSs whose obligations are calculated in hard Swiss currency. Possible consequences could take the form of American opposition to any further dues increases or deliberate underreporting of total membership.

431. Like other international trade union bodies, some ITSs rely on special contributions beyond normal affiliation fees to finance certain activities, especially their organizing work in less developed countries. These are voluntary payments, and for a variety of reasons certain unions, notably the Scandinavian ones and those in the Netherlands, are usually more receptive to such appeals than others. Some ITSs, for example the Building and Woodworkers, always set aside a portion of their dues, in this case 15 out of 50 Swiss centimes per member per year, for activities in developing areas.

432. The Plantation Workers Secretariat is an exception to the rule of ITS financial self-sufficiency. It has always required a sizable subsidy from the ICFTU and will likely continue to need external financing for a long time to come in view of the poverty of most of its affiliates. World inflation has further aggravated its financial difficulties, on top of the contraction of the agricultural labour force and the diminishing number of union members in farmworkers' organizations.

433. Outside funding is an important additional source for work in Third World countries. Support for educational activities has been made available particularly by the ILO and by the foreign aid agencies of several governments in North America and Western Europe. This includes the U.S. Agency for International Development (AID) which has channelled funds for union leadership training and development programs to several secretariats through the overseas institutes of the AFL-CIO. The German, Dutch, and Scandinavian governments have made similar provisions. At an earlier time, the ICFTU, too, was one of the more significant financial supporters of ITS regional activities through its International Solidarity Fund. In recent years, however, the ICFTU has not had the funds to continue the subsidies. Some secretariats reject in principle all government financial support regardless of source or intermediary, while others are merely selective. Fear of tainted funds is the principal motive for some secretariats; others are concerned about potential dependence and loss of full control over their activities.

H. Publications

434. Most secretariats publish the proceedings of their congresses, the activity reports of their officers, one or several periodicals, occasional special reports, and from time to time topical circular letters. Where regional organizations exist, their publications must also be added to this list. The main periodical, often called newsletter or news bulletin, usually appears on a monthly basis, but for reasons of economy some are now issued at longer intervals or irregularly; a few have been discontinued altogether. Translation costs are an important factor since virtually every publication, except perhaps those intended for a region with a common language, such as Latin America, must be issued in two or more languages.

II. Aims and Activities

435. The advancement of the collective interests of their affiliates has always been the primary objective of the ITSs, although like trade unions in general they also include among their stated goals broader commitments such as the protection of human rights, the establishment of a just social order, and the struggle for peace and freedom. Allowing for inevitable variations between ITSs the major activities usually include

1. information and research services;
2. solidarity actions;
3. regional activities;
4. relations with intergovernmental agencies;
5. establishment of minimum standards;
6. development of strategies for dealing with multinational companies.

The last-named item is of major importance to only those ITSs whose territory includes substantial numbers of multinationals. That means the IMF, FIET, ICEF, and IUF, and to a somewhat lesser degree the ITGLWF, ITF, and PTTI.

A. Information and Research Services

436. The most common type of activity still consists of the collection and dissemination of information about employment conditions, wages, hours, innovations in collective bargaining, and changes in labour legislation that are likely to be of interest to member organizations. Only the very largest ITSs have the proper means to conduct their own research into the economics of the industry or industries for which they are competent. They depend, therefore, on their affiliates to supply them with newsworthy items, but they would very much like to see intergovernmental organizations, such as the ILO and OCED become more directly engaged in applied research of direct interest to unions. Some of the better equipped ITSs have begun to collect and disseminate information, sometimes computerized, on the terms of employment in the subsidiaries of large companies, especially multinational ones. Increasing attention is also being given to problems of health and safety at work.

437. For some ITSs certain kinds of problems necessarily become perennial preoccupations. Safety is always a top priority for the Miners' Secretariat. The conflicting interests of affiliates over international trade in textiles and manufactured garments is always a key problem, and probably an insoluble one, for the Textile, Garment, and Leather Workers. Securing the right to organize and bargain collectively for employees in the public sectors has long been a topic of major importance to the PSI and PTTI. For the International Transport Workers Union the most enduring problem has been the proliferation of ships flying under so-called flags of convenience. This term is in current usage to describe the practice of shipowners, including major oil companies, to register their ships in countries offering attractive terms of registration. The terms include low fees, low tonnage taxes or tax exemptions, savings on crew costs due to non-union operations and lower social insurance charges, and similar advantages.

B. Solidarity Actions

438. A rather different service is the mobilization of international support on behalf of an ITS affiliate involved in a domestic labour dispute. An example is the case of the Farah Manufacturing Company where the Amalgamated Clothing Workers Union in the United States enlisted its ITS – the Textile, Garment and Leather Workers Union – in extending the domestic consumer boycott to the international area. Whether such services make an effective contribution to the outcome is obviously beyond accurate assessment.

439. Those ITSs whose domain includes industries dependent on international markets must often exercise great caution in approaching economic policy issues. This is especially the case where high-cost and low-cost producer countries compete in international trade. In the future, the inevitable conflicts of interest between ITS affiliates that are the result of such competition are likely to increase, particularly as less developed countries begin to compete more aggressively and more massively in sectors that have traditionally provided employment for workers in industrialized countries. The traditional union response to competition among members – namely, pressure on employers to equalize wages and the terms of employment – will not be practicable in most situations because neither the governments nor the unions of the new producer countries will be content to give up the competitive edge gained by lower labour costs. Since there is no solution conceivable that could satisfy all the parties, some ITSs have sought refuge in proposals for international conferences where the participants, including the unions, would try to reach agreement on the terms of fair competition.

C. Regional Activities

440. For the last 20 to 25 years, most ITSs have conducted programmes of organization, education, and training in less developed countries, the so-called regional activities. In certain regards, this is the sort of work for which they are considerably better equipped than the global internationals (ICFTU, WFTU, WCL). The purpose has been to create or strengthen individual unions by meeting some elementary needs, such as training union officers in organizing and administrative work, getting basic research underway, promoting financial self-sufficiency, advising on matters of internal union government, encouraging mergers of dual or closely related unions, and supporting the enactment of fundamental labour legislation. To implement these programmes the ITSs have stationed their own representatives in target areas, have conducted regional seminars, have arranged for study trips abroad, and have established permanent regional conferences. In some ITSs the regional conferences have become important constituent elements of the internal structure.

441. On the whole, regional activities have moved rather slowly. The problems of union building are usually not easily resolved, and in many developing areas the governments are not well disposed toward the idea of tolerating strong and independent unions. Some regard unions as a threat to their political authority, while others consider unions to be an obstacle to rapid economic development. In a substantial number of countries the labour laws circumscribe union activities. Other hurdles to union inroads include illiteracy, employer hostility, high levels of unemployment, linguistic and tribal divisions, and the prevalence of corruption.

D. Establishment of Minimum Standards

442. The idea of universal minimum standards is of course embedded in the founding of the International Labour Organization (ILO), but because the norms which it has developed are only rarely intended to apply to a specific economic sector some ITSs have sought to develop a set of standards adapted to their own domain. For over two decades, the IGF has maintained both a 'program for minimum trade union claims' and a 'model agreement' which together contain most items that are subject to collective regulation in the graphical industry. A more recent drive for a uniform minimum is FIET's 'World Action Programme' which contains proposed standards on working hours, overtime, vacations, and other items. FIET intends to conduct regular reviews of implementation, but success is doubtful. Standards set at levels that are challenging to unions in advanced countries are likely to be unattractive for unions in less developed countries. On the other hand, standards that are within the reach of unions in less developed countries are not likely to be of much concern to unions in industrialized countries.

E. Relations with International Agencies

443. Most ITSs maintain close contacts with intergovernmental organizations, especially with the International Labour Organization and its Industrial Committees. The ILO's general mandate to establish international labour standards is of interest to all segments of the international trade union movement, including the ITSs, but the work of the tripartite Industrial Committees is of special interest to the ITSs because these committees afford an opportunity to reach an international consensus on the standards that ought to prevail in a particular industry. ILO Industrial Committees cannot adopt binding regulations, but they may pass resolutions and adopt conclusions on agenda items that call for action by employers, governments, trade unions, or the ILO itself. Because of the tripartite composition of Industrial Committees, a certain amount of bargaining is expected on controversial agenda items, and out of this process there has emerged over the years a set of agreed resolutions, industry by industry, which may cover such items as maximum hours of work, minimum wages, safety rules, vocational and apprenticeship training, employment stabilization, job classification, productivity, and labour-management relations. During meetings of Industrial Committees it is the special responsibility of the appropriate ITS to brief the representatives from its own affiliated organizations and to act as a coordinating body for them, to prepare documentation in support of their proposals, and to assure that the ILO follows up on the conclusions and resolutions adopted at the meetings. Most ITSs are strong advocates of the Industrial Committee structure because it offers an unusual opportunity to define voluntary international guidelines for labour conditions and labour relations according to the special circumstances of an industry, and because of the important role which employee representatives occupy in that process.

F. Multinational Companies

444. As indicated above, support of the bargaining objectives of their affiliates has traditionally been one of the principal functions of the ITSs. But it has only been within the past two decades that the underlying work has moved beyond information exchanges, financial assistance for struggling affiliates, international solidarity actions, and efforts to prevent strike-breaking. In fact, for many ITSs these tasks are still central to their activities, but for others the growth of the multinational company has opened up new dimensions and new opportunities.

445. In some instances the initiative for ITS involvement in the problem of multinational companies has come mainly from national affiliates. This was the case in the IMF where the United Automobile Workers, an American affiliate, promoted the establishment of world auto councils already in the 1950s as a parallel structure to the principal worldwide corporations in the industry. In other cases, as for instance in the ICEF, the moving force came mainly from within the secretariat itself.

446. The creation of corporation councils has been the most visible response of some ITSs. The most active ITS in this regard, though not the only one, has been the IMF. Under the aegis of its Automotive Department, such councils have been established for eleven of the world's major automobile producers to facilitate cooperation between unions whose members work in the plants of these corporations. Other IMF departments – as well as other ITSs – have adopted the same institutional structure for industries in their areas of interest and have formed corporation councils or similar working parties to concentrate attention on particular firms in their industrial sector.

447. The activities of the world auto councils are also reasonably representative of similar bodies in other segments of the IMF and in other ITSs. In the first place they serve to facilitate a certain amount of liaison among unions of the same company in different countries, especially with regard to the timing, substance, and progress of collective bargaining. New agreements are circulated so as to make the new terms known to unions that will themselves sooner or later be engaged in negotiations with the same company.

448. Second, in the event the negotiations break down and a strike ensues, the council's coordinating work at IMF headquarters will aim at mobilizing solidarity actions by unions in other parts of the company. Under certain circumstances and particularly in less developed countries, such solidarity actions may have a considerable influence on the outcome of the dispute, especially if a strong, dominant union at company world headquarters intervenes on behalf of its counterpart in the outlying subsidiary.

449. Third, the very existence of a council tends to focus attention on disparities in the terms of employment between the subsidiaries of the same company, thus stimulating union attempts to achieve uniformity and to capitalize on gains already made elsewhere in the enterprise. While this does not constitute multinational bargaining, it does introduce a new dimension into the relationship between a multinational company and its subsidiaries on one hand and the organizations representing its employees on the other.

450. Other important ITS activities in the area of multinational companies have consisted of support for the development of guidelines by intergovernmental agencies (OECD, ILO, UN) and of participation, jointly with the ICFTU, in the drafting of a Charter of Trade Union Demands for the Legislative Control of Multinational Companies, as adopted at the ICFTU's Mexico City Congress in 1975. The formulation of guidelines has set the stage for unions, including the ITSs, to file claims alleging infractions or non-observance by multinational employers. At the very least such claims and the surrounding publicity serve to embarrass the company involved.

451. While developments at European level may eventually set the stage for the emergence of transnational bargaining within the European area, their exentension to broader geographic groupings that would involve the ITSs in actual negotiations with employers is not likely in the foreseeable future. Employers are generally opposed to such developments. Moreover, although national unions sometimes solicit ITS assistance in relations with employers, they have not demonstrated any readiness to cede authority or resources to the ITSs in amounts required for transnational bargaining. Other obstacles include inter-country differences in bargaining structures and traditions, the absence of a supranational legal framework, the awkward position of state-owned enterprises, and the potential contradictions between transnational bargaining and the maintenance of national wage policies.

452. Nevertheless one should not rule out developments that, while falling short of involving the ITSs in transnational bargaining, will bring them into closer rapport with employers. Beyond greater activity in support of the bargaining objectives of their national affiliates they may also become to some extent direct participants in the shaping of industrial policies. Several ITS officials at the rank of general secretary and assistant general secretary have been chosen by German unions to fill employee seats on the corporate supervisory boards under the German system of codetermination. For the most part the companies involved are German subsidiaries of American multinationals. In their capacity as board members, the ITS officials have at the very least an opportunity to raise issues which are not far removed from what would be likely subjects of transnational bargaining.

453. If present trends continue to further the eventual emergence of an international industrial relations system with its own sets of rules (guidelines) and appropriate actors, the position of the ITSs in the constellation of international trade uninionism will become steadily more important. Generally speaking, the ITSs are equipped better than any other conceivable trade union bodies to represent the job-oriented international interests of employees vis-à-vis employers and most public agencies. Moreover their emphasis on economic issues, as distinguished from political or ideological ones, confers on them a high degree of acceptability. Thus the prospects for international trade unionism are probably linked more closely to the ITSs than to any of the other organizations reviewed in this volume.

454. International Trade Secretariats

	Headquarters	Number of Members	Number of Affiliates	Number of Countries	Year
International Federation of Building and Woodworkers (IFBWW)	Geneva, Switzerland	3,000,000	110	55	1979
International Federation of Chemical, Energy, and General Workers' Unions (ICEF)	Geneva, Switzerland	5,500,000	110	66	1978
International Federation of Commercial, Clerical and Technical Employees (FIET)	Geneva, Switzerland	6,400,000	179	80	1979
Universal Alliance of Diamond Workers (UADW)	Antwerp, Belgium	11,000	4	4	1974
International Secretariat of Entertainment Trade Unions (ISETU)	Vienna, Austria	350,000	67	35	1978
International Union of Food and Allied Workers' Associations (IUF)	Geneva, Switzerland	1,800,000	167	60	1979
International Graphical Federation (IGF)	Berne, Switzerland	660,000	34	25	1979
International Federation of Journalists (IFJ)	Brussels, Belgium	83,000	28	25	1978
International Metalworkers' Federation (IMF)	Geneva, Switzerland	13,700,000	168	70	1979
Miners' International Federation (MIF)	London, England	1,200,000	35	32	1979
International Federation of Plantation, Agricultural and Allied Workers (IFPAAW)	Geneva, Switzerland	1,600,000	76	50	1977
Postal, Telegraph, and Telephone International (PTTI)	Geneva, Switzerland	3,300,000	174	86	1978
Public Services International (PSI)	Feltham, England	6,000,000	180	67	1978
International Federation at Free Teachers' Unions (IFFTU)	Brussels, Belgium	3,000,000	62	52	1979
International Textile, Garment and Leather Workers' Federation (ITGLWF)	Brussels, Belgium	5,400,000	130	63	1979
International Transport Workers Federation (ITF)	London, England	4,400,000	400	90	1979

455. Trade Union Internationals of the Worl Federation of Trade Unions

Trade Unions International of Agricultural, Forestry and Plantation Workers	Prague, Czechoslovakia
Trade Unions International of Workers of the Building, Wood and Building Materials Industries	Helsinki, Finland
Trade Unions International of Chemical, Oil and Allied Workers	Budapest, Hungary
Trade Unions International of Workers of the Food, Tobacco and Beverages Industries and Hotel, Cafe and Restaurant Workers	Sofia, Bulgaria
Trade Unions International of the Textile, Clothing, Leather and Fur Workers	Prague, Czechoslovakia
Trade Unions International of Metal and Engineering Workers	Prague, Czechoslovakia
Miners' Trade Unions International	Prague, Czechoslovakia
Trade Unions International of Public and Allied Employees	Berlin, German Democratic Republic
World Federation of Teachers' Unions	Prague, Czechoslovakia
Trade Unions International of Workers in Commerce	Prague, Czechoslovakia
Trade Unions International of Transport Workers	Prague, Czechoslovakia

456. International Trade Federations of the World Confederation of Labor

World Federation of Trade Unions of Non-Manual Workers	Antwerp, Belgium
World Federation of Building and Woodworkers Unions	Utrecht, Netherlands
World Organization for Energy, Chemical, and Miscellaneous Industries	Brussels, Belgium
International Federation of Trade Unions of Employees in Public Service	Brussels, Belgium
International Federation of Trade Unions of Transport Workers	Brussels, Belgium
International Federation of Textile and Garment Workers	Ghent, Belgium
International Christian Federation of Trade Unions of Graphical and Paper Industries	Amsterdam, Netherlands
World Federation of Agricultural Workers	Brussels, Belgium
World Federation for the Metallurgic Industry	Brussels, Belgium
International Federation of Christian Miners' Unions	Brussels, Belgium
World Federation of Workers in the Food, Drink, Tobacco and Hotel Trades	Brussels, Belgium
World Confederation of Teachers	Brussels, Belgium

Bibliography

457.

PERIODICALS

Free Labour World (ICFTU)
Labour (WCL)
World Trade Union Movement (WFTU)

BOOKS

BELING, WILLARD A., *Pan-Arabism and Labor* (Cambridge: Harvard University Press, 1960).

HAWKINS, CARROLL, *Two Democratic Labor Leaders in Conflict: The Latin American Revolution and the Role of the Workers* (Lexington, Mass.: D. C. Heath and Company, 1973).

LORWIN, LEWIS L., *The International Labor Movement: History, Policies, Outlook* (New York: Harper, 1953).

MIOTTO, ROBERTO, *Les Syndicats Multinationaux* (Rome: Instituto per l'Economia Europea, 1976).

PIEHL, ERNST, *Multinationale Konzerne und Internationale Gewerkschaftsbewegung* (Frankfurt: Europäische Verlagsanstalt, 1973).

SNOW, SINCLAIR, *The Pan-American Federation of Labor* (Durham, N.C.: Duke University Press, 1964).

WEDIN, AKE, *International Trade Union Solidarity: ICFTU 1957–1965* (Stockholm: Prisma, 1974).

WINDMULLER, JOHN P., *American Labor and the International Labor Movement, 1940 to 1953* (Ithaca, N.Y.: Cornell University, 1954).

ARTICLES AND ESSAYS

Cox, Robert W., 'Labor and Transnational Relations', *International Organization*, Vol. 25, No. 3 (Summer 1971), pp. 554–584.

Landsberger, Henry A., 'Linkages to World Society – International Labor Organizations in the Western Hemisphere', in Yale H. Ferguson (ed.), *Contemporary Inter-American Relations* (Englewood Cliffs: Prentice-Hall, 1972).

Roberts, B. C. and Bruno Liebhaberg, 'The European Trade Union Confederation: Influence of Regionalism, Detente and Multinationals', *British Journal of Industrial Relations*, Vol. 14, No. 3 (November 1976), pp. 261–273.

Windmuller, John P., 'European Regionalism: A New Factor in International Labour', *Industrial Relations Journal*, Vol. 7, No. 2 (Summer 1976), pp. 35–48.

Windmuller, John P., 'Realignment in the ICFTU: The Impact of Detente', *British Journal of Industrial Relations*, Vol. 14, No. 3 (November 1976), pp. 247–260.

Index

The numbers given refer to paragraphs.